A Christian Chronology Of History

A Time Line Of Human History
From A Christian Prospective

"God's Friend"

Order this book online at www.trafford.com
or email orders@trafford.com

Most Trafford titles are also available at major online book retailers.

Printed in the United States of America.

ISBN: 978-1-4269-5603-4 (sc)

Trafford rev. 01/17/2011

 www.trafford.com

North America & international
toll-free: 1 888 232 4444 (USA & Canada)
phone: 250 383 6864 ♦ fax: 812 355 4082

IF YOU WOULD LIKE TO HELP
THE CAMBODIAN MISSION EFFORT
MENTIONED IN THESE PAGES FOLLOWING 2000 A.D.
PLEASE CONTACT:
Cambodian Missions
Melrose Church of Christ
340 North 8th St.
Melrose, N.M., 88124

Before we get into the time chronology, I would like to describe some principles and basic understandings that have lead me to challenge some dates I confidently consider inaccurate though politically correct. If you believe that the Bible, as originally delivered, is the infallible word of God, and I do, then you expect the Bible to accurately describe historic events. If some human has decided to disagree with the Bible, I may pity his error, but will not knowingly join his folly. Some of the secular scholars' misunderstandings comes from a failure to understand the religious Jewish calendar used in the Bible, and failure to completely read ancient historians and the Bible. Often ancient historians do not know what they think they know and they always know incompletely. The same is true of modern historians. To help us in the discovery of an accurate, though grossly incomplete chronology from a Christian prospective, I am first introducing you to some notes on the Jewish religious calendar and the ending of Herod the Great's life. Herod's death has a lot to do with the proper dating of Jesus' birth, life, and death, an important Christian series of events that have been misdated by many.

NOTES ON THE JEWISH
RELIGIOUS CALENDAR

The Jewish calendar is not understood, or is misunderstood in the literature. Secular scholars worry too much about tying things to the things in the second heaven and ignore plain statements. This limits the accuracy of the available information. Much of what you read belongs in file thirteen and can best be described as mounds of misinformation with small amounts of imbedded truth. Most refer to the Jewish month as a lunar month and designate them as being 29 and 30 days. The 29 and 30 day lengths will not even grant a semblance of accuracy to even a most backward people. Over the course of a year all would note the counts failure to conform to the phases of the moon. A lunar cycle is 27.321661 days long, or about 27 1/3 days. In one year you become over a whole cycle off. The Bible describes months as being 30 days long. Bible years normally consist of twelve thirty day months that are 360 days long, but at times some years are 390 days long.

Some "authorities" have said that an extra month was added to the year about every three years to adjust the calendar of lunar months to the solar year. I believe these "authorities" never did the math involved in the adjustment they are claiming. A solar year is about 365.25636 days long. If you add 30 days every three years to the Bible's normal 360 day year, you are long over 237 days in a fifty year period, and that is cumulative. That did not happen.

The Bible calendar does function on a fifty year Jubilee cycle with years 7, 14, 21, 28, 35, 42 and 49 being special Sabbath years. The fiftieth year is a very special year of Jubilee (Lev. 25). If the Sabbath years and the year of Jubilee are given extra 30 day months, the fifty year cycle is less than 23 days off from the natural solar calendar. I feel certain that is what happened.

Some "authorities" suggest that at some unknown times 7 or 8 days were also added to the three annual festivals. If you add an eight day period to two of the annual festivals on the year of Jubilee and a seven day period to the third annual festival of that year, the Bible calendar would be off from the solar calendar by less than 4 ½ hours over a fifty year period. That is more accurate than our modern day solar calendar. I believe that is what was done.

Some pretend the three annual festivals were always the same number of days apart. That is not so. The Passover and the Feast of tabernacles were always on the same date on the Jewish Ceremonial calendar. Because of the calendar adjustments described above, those dates moved about by as much as seventy-one days on our calendar. The Pentecost Festival was tied to the Barley harvest and moved less on our calendar due to its dating being largely controlled by the natural solar calendar. That means it shifted in its relationship to the Passover by over two months during the fifty year cycle.

NOTE ON HEROD THE GREAT

Another area of misinformation in the literature is about the death of Herod the Great. According to Josephus, there was an eclipse the night Herod removed Matthias from the High Priesthood and burnt alive another Matthias, a teacher of the Law. This eclipse can be dated as March the 13th in 4 B.C. Many give that as the date of Herod's death, but it is merely a date from which Josephus says his sickness became worse.

After that date he sought medical assistance and traveled beyond the Jordan to bath in the warm baths at Calirrhoe. He then returned to Jericho and summoned and arrested many Jewish leaders. Herod acknowledged he was dying and wanted the community leaders killed at his death so there would be massive mourning at that time. He later received communications, Caesar announcing the execution of Acme and giving Herod permission to execute Antipater. Herod executed Antipater five days before his own death. Herod was dead by the Passover in 3 B.C. (March or April on our calendar, the 14th of the first month on the Jewish calendar). The story told by Josephus suggests to me that this Passover was very close to Herod's death. It was before Archelaus, Herod's heir apparent, sailed for Rome to have his inheritance validated by Caesar, something I believe he would do as soon as possible.

Table of Contents

CHAPTER ONE
A CHRISTIAN CHRONOLOGY OF HISTORY
(CREATION-2231 B.C.)
A TIME LINE OF HUMAN HISTORY
FROM A CHRISTIAN PROSPECTIVE
Compiled by "God's Friend"

4179 B.C.	CREATION:EVE'S SEED PROPHESIED TO CRUSH SATAN'S HEAD (SEE 7 B.C.) (Genesis 3:15; 5:1-3)
4174 B.C.	CAIN'S BIRTH
4173 B.C	ABEL'S BIRTH
4049 B.C.	SETH'S BIRTH (Genesis 5:3, 6)
3944 B.C.	ENOS'S BIRTH (Genesis 5:6, 9)
3854 B.C.	CAINAN'S BIRTH (Genesis 5:9, 12)
3784 B.C.	MAHALALEEL'S BIRTH (Genesis 5:12, 15)
3719 B.C.	JARED'S BIRTH (Genesis 5:15, 18)
3557 B.C.	ENOCH'S BIRTH (Genesis 5:18, 21)
3492 B.C.	METHUSELAH'S BIRTH (Genesis 5: 21, 25)
3305 B.C.	LAMECH'S BIRTH (Genesis 5:25, 28-29)
3249 B.C.	ADAM'S DEATH
3137 B.C.	SETH'S DEATH
3123 B.C.	NOAH'S BIRTH
2623 B.C.	JAPHETH'S BIRTH
2621 B.C.	SHEM'S BIRTH
2523-2522 B.C.	NOAH'S FLOOD: IN ABOUT MAY (THE MONTH OF THE FLOWERS), THE EARTH IS STRUCK BY A COMET (AN ICE STORM FROM OUTER SPACE). THE CRUST IS MOVED ABOUT FIVE THOUSAND MILES TO THE EAST IN RELATIONSHIP TO THE EARTH'S CORE. THE PACIFIC OCEAN IS SPLASHED OUT OF ITS BASIN AND

WASHED OVER CANADA. SHOCK WAVES
ENCOUNTERED MAJOR RESISTANCE
IN THE MIDDLE OF THE ATLANTIC
AND CRACKED THE CRUST FROM
THE ARCTIC TO THE ANTARTIC. THE
CRUST FOLDED LIKE AN ACCORDION
LEAVING MAGNETIC STRIPES OF
MOUNTAINOUS
MATERIAL ON BOTH SIDES OF THE
CRACK (MID-ATLANTIC RIFT). THE
EARTH'S CRUST CRACKED INTO ABOUT
TWENTY LARGE PIECES. ICE FROM
THE COMET CREATED GLACIERS ON
THE SLOPES OF TROPICAL ISLANDS
AND FORMED OUR CURRENT
POLAR ICE CAPS ATOP TROPICAL
JUNGLE. HERDS OF GIANT ELEPHANTS
(MAMMOTHS) WERE QUICK FROZEN
AS THEY MUNCHED ON BLOOMING
BUTTERCUPS.
THE EARTH WAS TILTED ON ITS AXIS BY
THE FORCE OF THE IMPACTS. MAGMA
WAS DRIVEN UP FROM THE MANTEL
AND BOILED THE GROUND WATER,
DRIVING IT INTO THE ATMOSPHERE.
THE INCOMING, SUPER COLD ICE,
PRECIPITATED ALL MOISTURE OUT
OF THE ATMOSPHERE. HEAVY METALS
WERE SPLASHED UP FROM THE MANTEL
INTO THE CRUST SURROUNDING THE
NORTH PACIFIC IMPACT AREA. HEAVY
METALS WERE ALSO SPLASHED UP
INTO THE CRUST MATERIAL ON THE
OPPOSITE SIDE OF THE PLANET (IN
AFRICA). THE CLIMATE IS CHANGED SO
THAT WHAT USE TO BLOOM IN APRIL
OR MAY IN THE RAIN FORESTS IS NOW
BLOOMING IN JULY. THE ENVIRONMENT
IS SO CONTAMINATED THAT MAN'S

LIFE EXPECTANCY IS REDUCED TO A TENTH OF THAT BEFORE THE FLOOD. THE PACIFIC OCEAN FLOOR IS DRIVEN UNDER SURROUNDING CONTINENTS. MOST FOSSILS ARE FORMED.

2522 B.C.   THE DESCENDANTS OF CANAAN, A SON OF HAM, A SON OF NOAH, IS PROPHESIED TO BECOME THE SLAVE OF SLAVES (SEE 1461 B.C.). HAM'S DESCENDANTS SETTLE AFRICA. THE DESCENDANTS OF SHEM (ISRAELITES, ARABS, AND SOUTHERN-CENTRAL ASIANS) ARE TO BE BLESSED WITH A SPECIAL RELATIONSHIP WITH GOD. (THEY ARE USED BY GOD TO WRITE THE BIBLE AND PROVIDE THE LINEAGE OF JESUS. ALL THE BIBLE PROPHETS AND APOSTLES COME FROM THIS LINE.) THE DESCENDANT S OF JAPHETH (EUROPEANS AND NORTH ASIANS) ARE TO HAVE THEIR TERRITORIES EXTENDED, AND COME TO LIVE IN SHEM'S HOUSE. (THE TERRITORIES CONTROLLED BY THIS GROUP TODAY INCLUDES ALL OF EUROPE, MOST OF ASIA, A LARGE PART OF AFRICA, ALL OF NORTH AND SOUTH AMERICA, AUSTRALIA, ICELAND, GREENLAND, AND NUMEROUS ISLANDS. MOST OF THOSE WHO CALL THEMSELVES CHRISTIANS OR CATHOLICS ARE FROM THIS GROUP. ACCORDING TO NEW TESTAMENT DOCTRINE, TODAY THE CHRISTIANS HAVE THE SPECIAL RELATIONSHIP THAT USE TO BE HELD BY THE JEWS. THEY ARE THE NEW ISRAEL, PRINCES OF GOD. (Galatians 4:21-31; 5:4,18; 6:15,16; Ephesians 2:11-14,18-22; Romans 8:14-17; 9:6-8; 24-27; 11:7-23; NOTE: Some Jews have chosen to

	become Christians and therefore still have their privileged relationship Matthew 21:33-46; 22:1-14; Mark 12:1-12; Luke 14:7-11; 15-24; 20:9-19)
2521 B.C.	ARPHAXAD'S BIRTH TWO YEARS AFTER THE FLOOD. (Genesis 11:10, 12)
2486 B.C.	SALAH'S BIRTH (Genesis 11:12, 14)
2456 B.C.	EBER'S BIRTH (Genesis 11:14, 16)
2422 B.C.	PEGLEG'S BIRTH (Genesis 11:16, 18)
2392 B.C.	REU'S BIRTH (Genesis 11:19, 20)
2360 B.C.	SEGAR'S BIRTH (Genesis 11:20, 22)
2350 B.C.	PEPI I DEFEATS REBELS AT THE GAZELLE'S HEAD IN THE VALLEY OF JEZREEL NEAR MEGIDDO.
2330 B.C.	NAHOR'S BIRTH (Genesis 11:22, 24)
2301 B.C.	TERAH'S BIRTH (Genesis 11:24, 26)
2231 B.C.	BIRTH OF ABRAHAM SHORTLY FOLLOWED OR ACCOMPANIED BY THE BIRTHS OF NAHOR AND HARAN Genesis 11:26; 11:10; 5:32).

CHAPTER TWO
A CHRISTIAN CHRONOLOGY OF HISTORY
(2231 B.C. – 1117 B.C.)
A TIME LINE OF HUMAN HISTORY
FROM A CHRISTIAN PROSPECTIVE
Compiled by "God's Friend"

2231 B.C.	**ABRAHAM'S BIRTH** **(Genesis 11:26, 21:5)**
2173 B.C.	**NOAH'S DEATH (Genesis 9:28)**
2156 B.C.	**ABRAM (ABRAHAM) SETS OUT FROM HARAN (Genesis 12:4)**
2154 B.C.	**ABRAM AND LOT COME TO CANAAN FROM EGYPT AND LOT SEPARATED TO SODOM AND GOMORRAH.**
2147 B.C.	**MELCHISEDEK BUILDS SALEM (JERUSALEM) VIA JOSEPHUS.**
2146 B.C.	**KEDORLAOMER, KING OF ELAM, CONQUERS THE SODOM AREA AND TAKES LOT PRISONER. ABRAM RESCUES.**
2145 B.C.	**ISHMAEL IS BORN.**
2145-2130 B.C.	**ISHMAEL AND HIS DESCENDANTS (ARABS) RECEIVE A BLESSING FROM GOD AT ABRAHAM'S REQUEST. HE IS TO PRODUCE 12 RULERS (KINGDOMS) AND BE GREATLY MULTIPLIED. HIS HAND WILL BE AGAINST EVERYONE, AND EVERYONE'S HAND WILL BE AGAINST HIM. HE WILL BE A WILD DONKEY OF A MAN. (SEE THE MODERN ARAB NATIONS AND THERE RECENT HISTORIES) GOD ALSO PROMISES TO ESTABLISH HIS COVENANT OF BLESSINGS THROUGH**

	ISAAC. (JESUS COMES THROUGH ISAAC). (Genesis 16:6-16; 17: 15-21)
2132 B.C.	HOMOSEXUAL SODOM AND GOMORRAH DESTROYED. (Genesis 17:1)
2131 B.C.	ISAAC'S BIRTH. (Genesis 21: 5)
2091 B.C.	ISAAC MARRIES REBEKAH. (Genesis 25:20)
2071 B.C.	ESAU AND JACOB'S BIRTH (Genesis 25:6)
2056 B.C.	ABRAHAM'S DEATH (Genesis 25:7, 8)
2021 B.C.	SHEM'S DEATH
1994 B.C.	JACOB LEAVES ISAAC AND REBECCA FOR HARAN AND LABAN'S HOUSEHOLD.
1980 B.C.	BIRTH OF JOSEPH NEAR HARAN
1974 B.C.	JACOB LEAVES HARAN AND LABAN'S HOUSEHOLD.
1963 B.C.	JOSEPH SOLD INTO EGYPT. (Genesis 37:2)
1951 B.C.	ISAAC'S DEATH (Genesis 35:28, 29)
1950 B.C.	JOSEPH BEGINS TO ADMINISTER EGYPT. (Genesis 41:46) (POSSIBLY UNDER SENUSRET I)
1941 B.C.	JACOB GOES TO EGYPT. (Genesis 47:9)
1941-1511 B.C.	JOB WRITTEN IN SAUDI ARABIA BY UNKNOWN AUTHOR.
1780-1591 B.C.	THE ISRAELITES ESTABLISH THEMSELVES AS A NATION IN THE LAND OF GOSHEN. (THE EASTERN NILE DELTA.) THEY ARE KNOWN TO THE EGYPTIANS AS HYKSOS.
1605-1595 B.C.	A NEW DYNASTY THAT IS OPPRESSIVE TOWARD THE ISRAELITES ESTABLISHES ITSELF IN EGYPT.
1591 B.C.	THE BIRTH OF MOSES (Under Intef VI or VII ?)
1511 B.C.	MOSES LEADS THE ISRAELITES OUT OF EGYPT AFTER 430 YEARS SOJOURN IN EGYPT (Under Thutmose I or Amenhotep I). (Exodus 12:40).

1510 B.C.	THE LAW IS RECEIVED AT MOUNT SINAI, THEN THE ISRAELITES MOVE TO KADESH-BARNEA. THEY SPY OUT THE LAND AND ARE CURSED WITH 40 YEARS WANDERINGS IN THE WILDERNESS FOR UNBELIEF.
1510-1471 B.C.	MOSES WRITES GENESIS, EXODUS, LEVITICUS, NUMBERS, AND DEUTERONOMY. HE PROPHESIED THAT THE MESSIAH WOULD COME FROM THE LINEAGE OF SHEM, ABRAHAM, ISAAC, JACOB, AND JUDAH. HE IS TO BE A PROPHET LEADER LIKE MOSES. WHOEVER DOESN'T LISTEN TO THE MESSIAH WILL HAVE TO ANSWER DIRECTLY TO GOD FOR THE INSULT. (SEE 7-1 B.C., 25-30 A.D., AND 70 A.D.) JUDAH WILL HAVE A KING AND LAWGIVER ON THE THROWN FOREVER.
1471 B.C.	DEATH OF MOSES, JOSHUA BEGINS CONQUEST OF CANAAN. THE CANAANITES ARE NEVER COMPLETELY DRIVEN OUT, BUT ARE USED FOR FORCED LABOR (JUDGES 1: 27-33).
1471-1470 B.C.	THE LAND IS DIVIDED BETWEEN THE TRIBES. CITIES OF REFUGE AND A GOVERNMENTAL SYSTEM OF LOCAL RULE AND AUTONOMY UNDER GOD IS ESTABLISHED AT GOD'S DIRECTION.
1471-1430 B.C.	THE WRITING OF JOSHUA
1457-1456 B.C.	THUTMOSE III, OF EGYPT, BARELY DEFEATS MESOPOTAMIAN HITITES AT MEGIDDO.
c1440-1433 B.C.	CHUSHRANISHATHAIM (Subbiliuliuma: to his own, "the Great King, the Noble King of Hatti." to Israel, "he of the two fold crimes of Chush.) ENSLAVES THE ISRAELITES.
c1433-1394 B.C.	OTHNIEL DELIVERS ISRAEL.
1421 B.C.	FIRST YEAR OF JUBILEE (Lev. 25)
c1394-1377 B.C.	EGLON OF MOAB ENSLAVES ISRAEL.
c1377-1298 B.C.	EHUD KILLS EGLON AND ISRAEL HAS REST

1371, 1321 B.C.	THE SECOND AND THIRD YEAR OF JUBILEE
c1298-1279 B.C.	JABIN OF CANAAN OPPRESSES ISRAEL.
c1279-1240	DEBORAH AND BARAK DEFEAT SISERA AT TAANACH AND MOUNT TABOR NEAR MEGIDDO. ISRAEL RESTS FOR 40 YEARS.
c1240-1234 B.C.	MIDIA TORMENTS ISRAEL.
c1234-1195 B.C.	GIDEON DEFEATS THE MIDIANITES AND AMALEKITES AT ENDOR AND MOREH. ISRAEL HAS 40 YEARS OF REST.
1221 B.C.	THE FIFTH YEAR OF JUBILEE
c1200 B.C.	TROY FALLS AND REFUGEES HELP ESTABLISH ROME. SAMUEL IS BORN.
c1195-1193 B.C.	ABIMELECH IS A TYRANT IN ISRAEL.
c1193-1171 B.C.	TOLA JUDGES ISRAEL. RUTH AND NAOMI RETURN TO BETHLEHEM.
c1182-1143 B.C.	THE PHILISTINES TORMENT ISRAEL.
c1172-1153 B.C.	SAMSON IS IN CONFLICT WITH THE PHILISTINES.
c1171-1150 B.C.	JAIR JUDGES ISRAEL.
1171 B.C.	THE SIXTH YEAR OF JUBILEE.
c1160-1143 B.C.	AMMON OPPRESSES ISRAEL.
c1143-1138 B.C.	JEPHTHAH DEFEATS AMORITES AND JUDGES ISRAEL
c1143 B.C.	ELI DIES AT 98 YEARS OLD AND HIS TWO SONS ARE KILLED. THE PHILISTINES TAKE THE ARK OF GOD AND THEN RETURN IT.
c1138-1132 B.C.	IBZAN JUDGES ISRAEL.
c1132-1123 B.C.	ELON JUDGES ISRAEL.
c1123-1117 B.C.	ABDON JUDGES ISRAEL.
c1123-1070 B.C.	THE PHILISTINES RENEW THEIR CONFLICT WITH ISRAEL.
1121 B.C.	THE SEVENTH YEAR OF JUBILEE

CHAPTER THREE
A CHRISTIAN CHRONOLOGY OF HISTORY
(1117 B.C. – 738 B.C.)
A TIME LINE OF HUMAN HISTORY
FROM A CHRISTIAN PROSPECTIVE
Compiled by "God's Friend"

1117-1075 B.C.	REIGN OF KING SAUL
c1100 B.C.	THE WRITING OF JUDGES
1110-1091 B.C.	SAMUEL PROBABLY WRITES RUTH AND THE FIRST 24 CHAPTERS OF 1 SAMUEL. SAMUEL REORGANIZES GOD'S PEOPLE FROM A SYSTEM BUILD AROUND LOCAL RULE AND AUTONOMY UNDER GOD, TO A HIGHLY CENTRALIZED KINGDOM SYSTEM. HE DID THIS AT THE INSISTENCE OF THE PEOPLE. THEY SAID THEY WANTED TO BE LIKE OTHERS AROUND THEM. GOD SAID THIS WAS A REJECTION OF GOD. GOD WARNED THEM OF MISERY THEY WERE CREATING, BUT PERMITTED IT AND CONTINUED TO WORK WITH THEM. (SEE 66-67, 380, 1776, 1787, AND 1992 A.D.)
1075 B.C	THE PHILISTINES DEFEAT SAUL AND JONATHAN AT MOUNT GILBOA NEAR MEGIDDO.
1071 B.C.	EIGHTH YEAR OF JUBILEE
1069 B.C.	KING DAVID CAPTURES JERUSALEM AND UNITES ISRAEL.
1069-1020 B.C.	NATHAN AND GAD WRITE REST OF 1 SAMUEL AND 2 SAMUEL.

1069-1041 B.C.	DAVID WRITES PSALMS, PROPHESYING THE MESSIAH WILL HAVE HIS HANDS AND FEET PIERCED AND SOLDIERS WILL DIVIDE HIS GARMENTS, CASTING LOTS FOR HIS VESTURE. HIS BODY WILL NOT BE LEFT IN GRAVE, BUT HE WILL BE RESURRECTED AND SEATED AT THE RIGHT HAND OF GOD. HE WILL BECOME A PRIEST LIKE MELCHIZEDEK. (SEE 28-30 A.D.) DAVID'S DESCENDANT WILL RULE ISRAEL (GOD'S PEOPLE: THE PEOPLE WHO HAVE POWER WITH GOD) FOREVER.
1043 B.C.	THE APPROXIMATE TIME THE CHILDREN OF ISRAEL QUIT HONORING JUBILEE AND SABBATH YEARS (RENT ON LAND OWED BY GOD).
1034 B.C.	SOLOMON BEGINS TO REIGN. 1031 B.C. CONSTRUCTION OF SOLOMON'S TEMPLE BEGINS. (1 Kings 6:1)
1021 B.C.	NINETH YEAR OF JUBILEE
1020-1006 B.C.	SOLOMON WRITES PROVERBS, SONG OF SOLOMON, AND ECCLESIASTES.
994 B.C.	DIVIDED KINGDOM (JUDAH-ISRAEL) BEGINS. (1 Kings 11:42)
994-978 B.C.	REHOBOAM RULES JUDAH (1Kings 14:21).
994 -973 B.C.	JEROBOAM 1ST RULES ISRAEL (1Kings 14:20).
986 B.C.	SHOSHENQ I (SHISHAK) DEFEATS MEGIDDO.
977-975 B.C.	ABIJAM RULES JUDAH (1 Kings 15:1, 2).
975-935 B.C.	ASA RULES JUDAH (1 Kings 15:9-10).
974-973 B.C.	NADAB RULES ISRAEL (1 Kings 15:25).
973-950 B.C.	BAASA RULES ISRAEL (1 Kings 15:33).
971 B.C.	TENTH YEAR OF JUBILEE
950-949 B.C.	ELAH RULES ISRAEL (1 Kings 16:8).

949 B.C.	ZIMRI KILLS ELAH AND RULES ISRAEL FOR 7 DAYS. THEN OMRI BESIEGES ZIMRI AND ZIMRI DIES. (1 Kings 16:15)
948-945 B.C.	CIVIL WAR IN ISRAEL BETWEEN OMRI AND TIBNI.
945-934 B.C.	OMRI RULES ISRAEL AND BUILDS SAMARIA (1 Kings 16:23-24).
938-917 B.C.	AHAB RULES ISRAEL (1 Kings 16:29).
935-911 B.C.	JEHOSHAPHAT RULES JUDAH (1Kings 22:42).
921 B.C.	ELEVENTH YEAR OF JUBILEE
919-918 B.C.	AHAZIAH RULES ISRAEL (1Kings 22:51).
918 B.C.	ELISHA WATCHES ELIJAH CARRIED TO HEAVEN BY A CHARIOT OF FIRE. (2Kings 2:11, 12)
918-907 B.C.	JEHORAM OF AHAB RULES ISRAEL (2 Kings 3:1).
919-914 B.C.	JEHORAM OF JEHOSHAPHAT HAS A CO-REGENCY IN JUDAH (2 Kings 8:16, 17; 2 Kings 1:17).
914-907 B.C.	JEHORAM'S FULL REGENCY IN JUDAH (2 KINGS 8:16)
910 B.C.	EDOM REBELLS FROM UNDER JUDAH (2 Kings 8:20; Genesis 27:38-40).
907 B.C.	AHAZIAH, JEHOSHAPHAT'S GRANDSON, RULES JUDAH (2 Kings 8:25, 26).
907 B.C	ELISHA HAS JEHU ANOINTED KING OVER ISRAEL. JEHU THEN KILLS JEHORAM OF AHAB AND AHAZIAH. AFTER JEHORAM IS WOUNDED BY THE SYRIANS AT JEZREEL NEAR MEGIDDO. HE SLAYS OR HAS SLAIN JEZEBEL AND ALL THE HOUSE OF AHAB ALONG WITH AHAZIAH AS PROPHESIED BY ELIJAH. HE ALSO SLAYS THE PRIESTS AND PROPHETS OF BAAL. (2 Kings Chapters 9, 10) HOWEVER, HE KEPT THE GOLDEN CALVES AT BETHEL AND DAN.

906-879 B.C.	JEHU RULES ISRAEL (2 Kings 10:36)
906-901 B.C.	ATHALIAH RULES JUDAH (2 Kings 11) SHE ATTEMPTS TO DESTROY THE LINEAGE OF DAVID. JOASH THE SON OF AHAZIAH SURVIVED, PROTECTED BY JEHOIADA THE PRIEST.
900-861 B.C.	JEHOASH (JOASH) RULES JUDAH (2Kings 12:1)
878-862 B.C.	JEHOAHAZ RULES ISRAEL (2Kings 13:1)
871 B.C.	THE TWELTH YEAR OF JUBILEE.
864-849 B.C.	JEHOASH, SON OF JEHOAHAZ, RULES ISRAEL (2Kings 13:10-25).
863-835 B.C.	AMAZIAH RULES JUDAH (2Kings 14:1, 2)
860 B.C.	AN UPRISING IN TYRE RESULTS IN THE KING'S DAUGHTER, ELISSA (DIDO), AND NOBLEMEN FROM TYRE FLEEING AND ESTABLISHING CARTHAGE IN AFRICA.
850 B.C.	HOMER WRITES THE ILIAD AND THE ODYSSEY
849-809 B.C.	JEROBOAM THE 2ND RULES ISRAEL. (2 Kings 14:23)
840 B.C.	JONAH WRITES JONAH. (2Kings 14:25)
823-772 B.C.	AZARIAH (UZZIAH) RULES JUDAH (2Kings 15:1-2)
821 B.C.	THE THIRTEENTH YEAR OF JUBILEE
825 B.C.	JOEL WRITES JOEL. HE PROPHESIES THERE WILL COME A TIME WHEN GOD POURS HIS SPIRIT OUT ON ALL NATIONS. MANY MIRACLES WILL BE DONE. WONDERS WILL BE SHOWN IN THE HEAVENS AND WHOEVER CALLS ON THE NAME OF THE LORD WILL BE SAVED. (SEE 29 A.D.)
820-725 B.C.	ISAIAH WRITES ISAIAH. HE PROPHESIES THE MESSIAH WILL NOT BE HANDSOME. HE WILL BE CALLED WONDERFUL COUNSELOR, MIGHTY GOD, EVERLASTING FATHER, PRINCE OF PEACE. HE WILL RULE ON DAVID'S

THROWN FOREVER. THERE WILL BE NO END TO THE INCREASE OF HIS GOVERNMENT AND PEACE. THE SPIRIT OF THE LORD WILL REST ON HIM. HE WILL STRIKE WITH THE ROD OF HIS MOUTH. PEACE WILL BE IN UNNATURAL PLACES AND THE EARTH WILL BE FULL OF THE KNOWLEDGE OF GOD. HE WILL BE FROM THE ROOT OF JESSE, A COVENANT FOR GOD'S PEOPLE, A LIGHT FOR THE GENTILES. HIS STRENGTH IS TO BE IN HIS MOUTH AND THE WORDS HE SPEAKS. HE WILL BE DESPISED, FORSAKEN, AND A MAN OF SORROW. HE WILL BRING GOOD TIDINGS. HIS TEACHINGS ARE TO BE GIVEN IN ZEBULUN AND NAPHTALI BY THE SEA, GALILEE OF THE NATIONS. HE WILL DO MANY MIRACLES. DESPITE ALL THESE SIGNS, THE PEOPLE WILL REJECT HIM.
HE IS TO BE LED LIKE A LAMB TO THE SLAUGHTER. THROUGH INJUSTICE HE IS TO DIE BEING ASSOCIATED WITH THE WICKED AND A RICH MAN IN HIS DEATH. HE WILL BE SLAIN FOR OUR INIQUITIES. A BOOK IS TO BE GIVEN TO LEAD PEOPLE OUT OF DARKNESS.
ALL NATIONS ARE TO FLOW INTO HIS KINGDOM. (SEE A.D. 28-30). THE ISRAELITE PEOPLE, BECAUSE OF THEIR SIN, WILL BE CARRIED OFF INTO SLAVERY, BUT WILL BE RETURNED TO START THE NATION AGAIN.
A PAGAN NAMED "CYRUS" WILL HELP ACCOMPLISH THE RETURN.

815 B.C.　AMOS WRITES AMOS. HE PROPHESIES THAT DAMASCUS WILL BE CONQUERED AND CARRIED INTO SLAVERY TO KIR.

	THE PHILISTINES SHALL PERISH. ISRAEL IS TO BE DESTROYED BY ASSYRIA (SEE 753-736, 608 B.C.)
800-740 B.C.	HOSEA WRITES HOSEA. HE PROPHESIES ISRAEL WILL BE SCATTERED AMONG THE NATION BECAUSE SHE HAS NOT BEEN FAITHFUL TO GOD. BECAUSE OF THEIR IGNORANCE ABOUT GOD THEY COME TO RUIN (SEE 737 AND 608 B.C.). THOSE THAT WERE NOT GOD'S PEOPLE WILL BE CALLED HIS PEOPLE (SEE 29 B.C.).
786 B.C.	ZACHARIAH RULES ISRAEL 6 MONTHS. HE IS KILLED BY SHALLUM WHO RULES ONE MONTH. SHALLUM IS KILLED BY MENAHEM.
785-776 B.C.	MENAHEM RULES ISRAEL (2 Kings 15:14-18).
774-773B.C.	PEKAHIAH RULES ISRAEL (2 Kings 15:23-26).
772-753 B.C.	PEKAH RULES ISRAEL (2 Kings 15:27-31).
771 B.C.	THE FOURTEENTH YEAR OF JUBILEE.
771-715 B.C.	MICAH WRITES MICAH. HE PROPHESIES THE MESSIAH WELL BE BORN IN BETHLEHAM (SEE 5 B.C.).
771-756 B.C.	JOTHAM RULES JUDAH (2 Kings 15: 32, 33).
757- 741 B.C.	AHAZ RULES JUDAH (2 Kings 16:1, 2).
756-730 B.C.	REZIN OF SYRIA AND PEKAH OF ISRAEL ATTACK AHAZ OF JUDAH. AHAZ CONTRACTS WITH ASSYRIA FOR HELP. ASSYRIA CONQUERS DAMASCUS AND CARRIES THE INHABITANTS INTO SLAVERY AT KIR. LATERASSYRIA ATTEMPTS TO CONQUER THE WHOLE REGION, CARRYING SAMARIA INTO SLAVERY AND DESTROYING ALL THE CITIES OF JUDAH BUT JERUSALEM. DIVINE INTERVENTION,

IN WHICH A HUNDRED AND EIGHTY-
FIVE THOUSAND ASSYRIANS DIE
IN ONE NIGHT, SAVES JERUSALEM.
FOUR DIFFERENT ASSYRIAN KING
PARTICIPATE IN THESE CAMPAIGNS,
TIGLATH-PILESER (PUL), SHALMANESER,
SARGON, AND SENNACHERIB.

746-738 B.C.   HOSEA RULES ISRAEL (2 Kings 17:1).

744-716 B.C.   HEZEKIAH RULES IN JUDAH
(2 Kings 18:1, 2).

738 B.C.   THE FALL OF SAMARIA TO SARGON
DURING HOSHEA'S REIGN IN ISRAEL.
SARGON CARRIES OFF THE NORTHERN
TRIBES.

CHAPTER FOUR
A CHRISTIAN CHRONOLOGY OF HISTORY
(738 B.C. – 604 B.C.)
A TIME LINE OF HUMAN HISTORY
FROM A CHRISTIAN PROSPECTIVE
Compiled by "God's Friend"

730 B.C.	THE DIVINE DEFEAT OF SENNACHERIB'S ARMY AT JERUSALEM DURING HEZEKIAH'S REIGN IN JUDAH. 185,000 DIE IN ONE NIGHT.
721 B.C.	FIFTEENTH YEAR OF JUBILEE
715-661 B.C.	MANASSEH RULES JUDAH. (2 Kings 21:1)
671 B.C.	SIXTEENTH YEAR OF JUBILEE
661-660 B.C.	AMON RULES JUDAH (2 Kings 21: 19).
660-630 B.C.	JOSIAH RULES JUDAH (2 Kings 22:1).
650-630 B.C.	NAHUM WRITES NAHUM. HE PROPHESIES THAT LIKE THE FALL OF THEBES, THE FALL OF ASSYRIA WILL BE AMAZING, TERRIBLE, AND UNMOURNED, BUT APPLAUDED BY MANY (SEE 630 B.C.).
648-607 B.C.	JEREMIAH WRITES LAMENTATIONS, 1 KINGS AND MOST OF JEREMIAH AND SECOND KINGS. DANIEL HAD ACCESS TO AT LEAST SOME OF JEREMIAH'S WRITINGS (Daniel 9), AND I BELIEVE, MADE A SMALL ADDITION TO THE ENDS OF JEREMIAH AND 2 KINGS. JEREMIAH PROPHESIED THAT GOD WOULD GIVE A NEW COVENANT OR TESTAMENT, NOT LIKE

THE ONE DELIVERED BY MOSES (SEE 29-96 A.D.).

GOD WLL PROVIDE A GOOD SHEPHERD FOR HIS PEOPLE. THIS SHEPHERD WILL LOOK AFTER GOD'S PEOPLE AS A SHEPHERD LOOKS AFTER HIS SHEEP. GOD WILL RAISE UP A RIGHTEOUS BRANCH FROM KING DAVID THAT WILL SAVE THE PEOPLE (SEE 5-29 A.D.). GOD WILL RETURN THE CAPTIVES FROM THE NORTH COUNTRY (SEE 536-444 B.C.). JERUSALEM AND ALL THE NEIGHBORING NATIONS WILL BE DESTROYED BY BABYLON (SEE 619-608 B.C.).

RESISTING BABYLON'S RULE WILL ONLY MAKE MATTERS WORSE. MOAB, AMMON, ELAM, JUDAH WILL BE RESTORED. BABYLON WILL BE MADE DESOLATE, SEVENTY YEARS AFTER THE DESOLATION OF JUDAH. THEN THE CAPTIVES WILL BE SENT HOME (SEE 608 B.C., 538 B.C., AND 536 B.C.).

647-626 B.C. NEBOPOLLASSAR RULES BABYLON (NEBUCHADNEZZAR'S FATHER). NOTE AS REGUARDS THE BABYLONIAN DYNASTY: THE BIBLE DATES NEBUCHADNEZZAR AND EVIL-MURDOCK. IT ALSO ENDORSES THE REIGN OF BELSHAZZAR, BUT HELPS DATE ONLY THE END OF THAT REIGN, INDICATING HE REIGNED AT LEAST THREE YEARS. JOSEPHUS LISTS THE KINGS IN THIS DYNASTY IN ORDER GIVING LENGTHS OF REIGN. THOSE LENGTHS ARE IMPOSSIBLE. HE ALSO FAILS TO MENTION NABONIDUS, BUT ATTRIBUTES A SIMILAR NAME TO BELSHAZZAR. A SIGNIFICANT COLLECTION OF CUNEIFORM

	TABLETS DOCUMENT THE CO-REGENCY OF BELSHAZZA AND HIS FATHER, NABONIDUS. I'VE MERGED INFORMATION ABOUT THE KINGS FROM JOSEPHUS, AND DR. E.J. YOUNG'S "THE PROPHECY OF DANIEL." I THEN USED WHAT SEEMED REASONABLE TO ME. I MUST ADMIT THAT THERE IS ARBITRARINESS IN SOME OF THE LENGTH'S AND THEREFORE DATES. HOWEVER, THE OVER ALL PERIOD OF BABYLONIAN CAPTIVITY IS RELIABLE AND VERIFIED BY JEREMIAH AND DANIEL.
645 B.C.	ZEPHANIAH WRITES ZEPHANIAH. HE PROPHESIES THE DESTRUCTION OF THE CITIES OF THE PHILISTINES, MOAB, AMMON, ETHIOPIA, AND ASSYRIA. NINEVEH IS TO BECOME COMPLETELY DESOLATE. A PURIFIED REMNANT OF ISRAEL AND JERUSALEM WILL BE PROTECTED (SEE 630-536 B.C.).
645 B.C.	EZEKIEL IS BORN.
630 B.C.	PHARAOH-NECHO IS REFUSED PASSAGE BY JOSIAH. JOSIAH IS SLAIN AT MEGIDDO. NECHO GOES TO FIGHT THE ASSYRIANS AT CHARCHEMISH ALLIED WITH THE BABYLONIANS. ASSYRIA IS DEFEATED AND LATER NINEVEH DESTROYED.
630 B.C.	JEHOAHAZ RULES JUDAH 3 MONTHS. (2 Kings 23:30-31)
629-627 B.C.	BABYLON INVADES JUDAH AND TAKE EVERYTHING FROM THE NILE TO THE EUPHRATES FROM EGYPT. DANIEL AND OTHERS ARE CARRIED INTO BABYLONIAN SLAVERY.
630-619 B.C.	HABAKKUK WRITES HABAKKUK. THE CALDEANS HAVE BEEN BROUGHT TO PUNISH THE NATION, BUT THEY

TOO SHALL BE PUNISHED FOR THEIR VIOLENCE (SEE 538 B.C.).

629-619 B.C.   EIIAKIM (JEHOIAKIM) RULES JUDAH (2 Kings 23:31-36).

627-583 B.C.   NEBUCHADNEZZAR RULES BABYLON.

627 B.C.   NEBUCHADNEZZAR ASSUMES COMMAND OF BABYLON'S ARMY AND SUBJUGATES JEHOIAHKIM AND OTHERS, TAKING DANIEL AND HIS FRIENDS CAPTIVE. DANIEL DATES HIS RULE FROM THIS DATE.

626 B.C.   NEBUCHADNEZZAR'S FATHER DIES IN BABYLON AND NEBUCHADNEZZAR RETURNS TO BABYLON TO BE RECOMFIRMED AS KING. HE THEN GOES TO A BATTLE AT CARCHEMISH WHERE HE DEFEATS THE EGYPTIANS. JEREMIAH DATES HIS RULE FROM HIS RECONFIRMATION AFTER HIS FATHER'S DEATH.

626 B.C.   DANIEL REVEALS AND INTERPRETS NEBUCHADNEZZAR'S DREAM OF THE GREAT IMAGE.

627-625 B.C.   JEHOIAKIM SERVES BABYLON AND THEN WITHOLDS TRIBUTE.

623-534 B.C.   DANIEL WRITES DANIEL. (NEBUCHADNEZZAR WRITES CHAPTER FOUR OF DANIEL). HE PROPHESIES PERSIA WILL CONQUER BABYLON (SEE 538 B.C.), GREECE WILL CONQUER PERSIA (SEE 336 B.C.), THE GREEK EMPIRE WILL BE DIVIDED INTO FOUR KINGDOMS (SEE 323 B.C.) THE ROMANS WILL CONQUER THE GREEK EMPIRE (SEE 168 B.C. TO 30 B.C.) AND DURING THE ROMAN RULE GOD WILL SET UP A KINGDOM (SEE 29-30 A.D.) THAT WILL GROW AND FILL THE EARTH. HE ALSO PROPHESIES THAT FROM A DECREE TO

RESTORE JERUSALEM TO THE MESSIAH'S (ETERNAL, WORLD KING'S) COMING WILL BE YEARS (SEE 458 B.C. AND 25 A.D.). THE MESSIAH WILL STAY FOR THREE AND A HALF YEARS AND THEN LEAVE (SEE 29 A.D.). THEN JERUSALEM WILL BE DESTROYED (SEE 70 A.D., 1 Chronicles 17: 11-15).

621 B.C.   THE SEVENTEENTH YEAR OF JUBILEE

619 B.C.   JEHOIACHIN AND 10,000 JERUSALEM CAPTIVES ARE REMOVED BY THE BABYLONIANS (NEBUCHADENZZAR). EZEKIEL IS INCLUDED IN THE CAPTIVES.

618-608 B.C.   ZEDEKIAH RULES JUDAH (2 Kings 24: 17, 18).

618-608 B.C.   EZEKIEL WRITES EZEKIEL. HE PROPHESIES   THAT THE CAPTIVES SHOULD WORK TO MAKE LIVES IN THE LAND THEY HAVE BEEN CARRIED TO BECAUSE JERUSALEM WILL NOT RISE UP AND FREE THEM. HE TELLS OF A MESSIAH THAT WILL BE A TEACHER, SHEPHERD OF GOD'S PEOPLE. HE ALSO PROPHESIES THAT IN A DISTANT TIME, IN THE LAST DAYS, THAT NATIONS (SOMALIANS OR SUDANIANS, IRANIANS, LIBYANS, GERMANIC PEOPLES, MONGOLIANS (POSSIBLY CHINA (SEE 1279 A.D.), AND A PEOPLE THAT LIVED NORTH OF THE GERMANS LEAD BY RUSSIA) WILL INVADE A LAND FULL OF PEOPLE WHO HAVE POWER WITH GOD (OR PRINCES OF GOD, SONS OF GOD-ISRAEL TRANSLATED). THEY WILL BE IN A VERY PROSPEROUS LAND THAT USE TO BE EMPTY, BUT IS NOW FULL OF PEOPLE. THEIR VILLAGES WILL NOT BE FORTIFIED. GOD'S PEOPLE WILL HAVE COME FROM MANY DIFFERENT NATIONS (SEE 1620

A.D.). THE SPANISH AND ARABS WILL BE BYSTANDERS. THE EVIL NATIONS WILL ATTACK SEEKING PLUNDER. GOD WILL DEFEND AND THE ATTACKING NATIONS WILL DIE IN A LARGE VALLEY EAST OF THE OCEAN WHERE TRAVELERS GO. THE INVADING NATIONS WILL BE DESTROYED BY FAMINE, DISEASE, INTERNAL FIGHTING, AND FIRE, HAIL, AND RAIN FROM THE SKY (SEE 57 A.D., 96 A.D., 2000 A.D., AND AFTERWARDS).

610-604 B.C.   NEBUCHADNEZZAR BESIEGES JERUSALEM, DESTROYS IT AND CARRIES OFF CAPTIVES AGAIN. THE REMAINING JUDEANS KILL THE LEADER APPOINTED BY THE BABYLONIANS AND RUN OFF TO EGYPT. JEREMIAH IS FORCED TO GO WITH THEM.

608 B.C.   ZEDEKIAH IS CAPTURED, HIS SONS ARE SLAIN BEFORE HIM AND HIS EYES ARE PUT OUT.
JERUSALEM AND ALL THE HOMES THERE ARE BURNT TO THE GROUND. THE FIRST TEMPLE, BUILT BY KING SOLOMON, IS DESTROYED BY NEBUCHADNEZZAR (SEE JEREMIAH 3:12; 2 KINGS 25:8, 9).

606 B.C.   OBADIAH WRITES OBADIAH. HE PROPHESIES THE DESOLATION OF EDOM BECAUSE OF ITS REJOICING IN THE DESTRUCTION OF JUDAH. AT THIS TIME EDOM IS A SIGNIFICANT PEOPLE TO THE SOUTHEAST OF JUDAH. BY THE TIME OF CHRIST THEIR LAND IS DESOLATE.

CHAPTER FIVE
A CHRISTIAN CHRONOLOGY OF HISTORY
(604 B.C. – 27 B.C.)
A TIME LINE OF HUMAN HISTORY
FROM A CHRISTIAN PROSPECTIVE
Compiled by "God's Friend"

591-585 B.C.	THE PROBABLE YEARS OF NEBUCHADNEZZAR'S INSANITY (Daniel 4).
582-565 B.C.	EVILMERODACH RULES BABYLON. HE TAKES JEHOICHIN FROM PRISON GIVING HIM AN ALLOWANCE FOR THE REST OF HIS LIFE (Jeremiah 52:31-34; 2 Kings 25:27-30).
571 B.C.	EIGHTEENTH YEAR OF JUBILEE
565-561 B.C.	NEGLISSAR (NERIGLISAR) RULES BABYLON.
563 B.C.	BIRTH OF SIDDHARTHA GAUTAMA, FOUNDER OF THE BUDDHIST SECTS. HE IS BORN IN INDIA NEAR A REGION UNDER PERSIAN CONTROL.
560 B.C.	LABOSORADACUS RULES BABYLON FOR NINE MONTHS.
560-538 B.C.	NABONIDAS (NABOANDELUS) RULES BABYLON.
554-538 B.C.	BELSHAZZAR (BALTASAR) RULES BABYLON.
554 B.C.	DANIEL HAS A VISION OF FOUR BEASTS.
552 B.C.	DANIEL HAS A VISION OF A TWO HORNED RAM AND A ONE HORNED GOAT.

538 B.C.

BELSHAZZAR SEES THE HAND WRITING ON THE WALL AND PROMISES A THIRD OF HIS KINGDOM OR THE THIRD RANK IN THE KINGDOM TO ITS INTERPRETER.

538-536 B.C.

AFTER JERUSALEM HAS BEEN DESOLATE FOR SEVENTY YEARS, BABYLON IS DESTROYED AS PROPHESIED (2 Chronicles 36:16-23; Jeremiah. 25:8-14; 29:10; 52:12-34; Daniel 9:1-19). THE FALL OF BABYLON TO THE MEDO-PERSIANS (DARIUS THE MEDE RULES). DANIEL IS THROWN IN THE LIONS' DEN. WHEN HE SURVIVES, DARIUS ORDERS "THAT IN ALL THE DOMINION OF HIS KINGDOM MEN ARE TO TREMBLE AND FEAR BEFORE THE GOD OF DANIEL...." DANIEL BECOMES CHIEF ADMINISTRATOR OF THE ENTIRE EMPIRE. DANIEL PROPHESIES THE COMING OF THE GREAT MESSIAH 483 YEARS AFTER THE ORDER THAT RESTORES JERUSALEM. DATING FROM EZRA'S ORDER TO GO TO JERUSALEM AND TEACH THE WORD OF GOD, IT IS 483 YEARS TO THE BAPTISM OF JESUS AND THE BEGINNING OF JESUS' PERSONAL MINISTRY. DANIEL SAYS THE MESSIAH WILL THEN LEAVE IN THREE AND A HALF YEARS. THREE AND A HALF YEARS AFTER JESUS' BAPTISM, JESUS IS CRUCIFIED, RESURRECTED, AND ASCENDS INTO HEAVEN. DANIEL THEN SAYS A PRINCE WILL COME AND DESTROY JERUSALEM. TITUS, SON OF THE EMPEROR OF ROME, DESTROYS JERUSALEM IN 70 A.D. DANIEL MAKES A WRITTEN RECORD OF THIS PROPHESY. DANIEL PREDICTS THE COMING OF THE MESSIAH IN ABOUT 500 YEARS. HE ALSO

	INDICATES THE 3 AND ½ YEARS WILL HAVE 1290 DAYS IN IT AND PENTICOST WILL BE 45 DAYS FROM THE DEATH OF JESUS. (SEE Daniel 12; 29 A.D.)
536 B.C.	CYRUS BEGINS TO RULE. CYRUS DECREES THAT JEWS MAY RETURN FROM CAPTIVITY TO REPOPULATE JERUSALEM AND REBUILD THE TEMPLE. (A fulfillment of Isaiah 44: 24-45 ...see 820-725 B.C.)
535 B.C.	FOUNDATION OF THE SECOND TEMPLE LAID.
534 B.C.	BUDDHA BEGINS TRAINING, HAVING BEEN ORDERED BY THE PERSIAN KING TO HONOR DANIEL'S GOD ABOVE ALL OTHERS. HE TEACHES HIS FOLLOWERS THAT THE HIGHEST GOD, CREATER OF EVERYTHING, THE LORD OF MERCIES (SI-A-MEETREY), WILL BE KNOWN AS LORD OF LORDS AND THE KING OF KINGS. HE WILL COME IN THE FUTURE. HE WILL BE THE ONLY ONE TO EVER BE ABLE TO FORGIVE SINS. HE WILL HAVE BLOODY HANDS AND FEET AND A HOLE IN HIS SIDE. HIS ARMY WILL CONQUER THROUGH LOVE AND COMPASSION. BUDDAH TELLS HIS FOLLOWERS TO LEAVE THEIR OLD WAYS AND JOIN HIS ARMY WHEN THE ARMY COMES TO THEIR LANDS. BUDDAH IS OBSESSED WITH SUFFERING, AGING, AND SICKNESS. HE SAYS THE WAY TO AVOID THESE EVILS IS TO NEVER BE BORN. SINCE HE BELIEVES IN REINCARNATION, HIS SOLUTION IS TO BE GOOD ENOUGH TO NOT HAVE TO BE REBORN AND CEASE TO EXIST.
529 B.C.	DEATH OF CYRUS.
529-521 B.C.	CAMBYSES RULES PERSIA.

522 B.C.	WORK ON THE SECOND TEMPLE STOPPED.
521 B.C.	NINETEENTH YEAR OF JUBILEE.
521 B.C.	SMERDIS (PSEUDO) RULES PERSIA. THIS APPEARS TO BE AN ATTEMPT BY THE MAGI (A SECT OF THE MEDES) TO REGAIN CONTROL OF THE EMPIRE. AFTER CAMBYSES REASSERTS HIS AUTHORITY, I BELIEVE THERE WAS A PURGING OF THE RECORDS TO REMOVE THE RECORD OF EARLY MEDE LEADERSHIP.
521-486 B.C.	DARIUS HYSTAPSIS (DARIUS I) REIGNS IN PERSIA .
520 B.C.	HAGGAI WRITES HAGGAI, WORK ON THE SECOND TEMPLE BEGINS AGAIN.
520-518 B.C.	FOUR MONTHS AFTER HAGGAI BEGINS PROPHESYING, ZECHARIAH BEGINS PROPHESYING AND WRITES ZECHARIAH. HE PROPHESIES THE SECOND DESTRUCTION OF JERUSALEM SHORTLY AFTER THE DEATH OF THE MESSIAH (SEE 70 A.D.). GOD'S PEOPLE WILL BEGIN DENYING THE GIFT OF PROPHESY TO LIMIT DECEIT. THE MESSIAH WILL HAVE A TRIUMPHANT ENTRY INTO JERUSALEM RIDING ON A COLT THE FOAL OF AN ASS. (SEE 25-29 A.D. AND 96 A.D.)
515 B.C.	THE SECOND JERUSALEM TEMPLE IS COMPLETED.
485-465 B.C.	XERXES RULES PERSIA. THIS IS THE EMPEROR OF PERSIA THAT ATTEMPTS THE CONQUEST OF GREECE AND MACEDONIA.
485 B.C.	XERXES SETS OUT TO INVADE GREECE FROM SARDIS.
483 B.C.	BUDDHA DIES. HE HAS TOLD HIS FOLLOWERS OF A COMING MESSIAH, "SIRA-ADIA-MEETREY," WHO HAS A

SCARED FOREHEAD, BLOODY HANDS
AND FEET AND A BLOODY SIDE. HE
IS THE PRINCE OF MERCY, KING OF
KINGS, AND LORD OF LORDS, WHO
CAN FORGIVE SINS. HIS ARMY IS TO
COME FROM THE WEST WITH WEAPONS
OF LOVE, COMPASSION AND MERCY.
BUDDHA TELLS HIS FOLLOWERS THAT
WHEN THEY COME THEY SHOULD LEAVE
THEIR OLD WAYS AND JOIN THEM. SIRA-
ADIA-MEETREY IS TO COME IN ABOUT
500 YEARS. BUDDHA DOES NOT WRITE
HIS TEACHINGS DOWN BUT THEY ARE
PASSED ON BY WORD OF MOUTH.

471 B.C.	TWENTIETH YEAR OF JUBILEE.
464-422 B.C.	ARTAXERXES LONGIMANUS RULES PERSIA. JOSEPHUS SAYS THAT THIS IS THE HUSBAND OF EASTER, AS DOES THE SEPTUAGINT.
462 B.C.	ESTHER IS CHOSEN AS SUCCESSOR FOR VASHTI, QUEEN OF PERSIA.
458 B.C.	DECREE IS ISSUED SENDING EZRA TO JERUSALEM TO TEACH THE BIBLE TO THE PEOPLE. SPIRITUAL RESTORATION OF JERUSALEM BEGINS.
456-445 B.C.	EZRA WRITES 1, 2 CHRONICLES AND EZRA.
453 B.C.	HAMAN PLOTS AGAINST THE JEWS. ESTHER INTERVENES AND MORDECAI BECOMES SECOND IN COMMAND IN THE PERSIAN EMPIRE. THE CELEBRATION OF PURIM BEGINS DURING THE 12th MONTH, ADAR.
452-450 B.C.	UNKNOWN AUTHOR WRITES ESTHER.
445-444 B.C.	NEHEMIAH SENT TO JERUSALEM TO REBUILD THE WALLS OF JERUSALEM.
440 B.C.	NEHEMIAH WRITES NEHEMIAH.
440 B.C.	MALACHI WRITES MALACHI. HE PROPHESIES THAT A PROPHET WOULD

	PREPARE THE WAY BEFORE THE MESSIAH (SEE 25 A.D.).
421 B.C.	TWENTY-FIRST YEAR OF JUBILEE.
422-404 B.C.	DARIUS II RULES PERSIA.
404-358 B.C	ARTAXERXES II RULES PERSIA.
371 B.C.	TWENTY-SECOND YEAR OF JUBILEE.
358-338 B.C.	ARTAXERXES III RULES PERSIA.
356 B.C.	ALEXANDER THE GREAT IS BORN.
338-336 B.C.	ARSES RULES PERSIA.
336-323 B.C.	ALEXANDER THE GREAT CONQUERS THE KNOWN WORLD. HE ORDERS JERUSALEM TO SEND HIM SUPPLIES. THEY REPLY THAT THEY CAN NOT COMPLY BECAUSE OF THEIR OATH TO THE PERSIAN EMPEROR, BUT WILL NOT FIGHT AGAINST HIM. HE MARCHES ON JERUSALEM. THEY OPEN THEIR GATES AND THE HIGH PRIEST IN HIS OFFICIAL ATTIRE GREETS ALEXANDER. ALEXANDER SAYS HE HAS HAD A VISION OF THE HIGH PRIEST AND GIVES THE JEWS SPECIAL TREATMENT BECAUSE OF DANIEL'S PROPHESIES.
336-331 B.C.	DARIUS III CODOMANNUS RULES PERSIA. HE IS DEFEATED BY ALEXANDER THE GREAT AT THE BATTLE OF GAUGAMELA (OR ARBELA).
334 B.C.	ALEXANDER INVADES ASIA MINOR.
323 B.C.	DEATH OF ALEXANDER THE GREAT ON MAY 21ST. HE DIVIDES HIS EMPIRE AMONG GREEK GENERALS PTOLEMY, CASSANDER, LYSMACHUS, AND SELEUCUS. PTOLEMY'S EMPIRE CENTERS IN EGYPT AND SELEUCUS' IN SYRIA. THEY ARE THE ONES WHO IMPACT PALESTINE. (SEE Daniel 7:6; 8:8, 22)
323-30 B.C.	THE PTOLEMY DYNASTY RULES EGYPT.

323-285 B.C.	PTOLEMY I (SOTER) RULES EGYPT (Daniel 11:5).
321 B.C.	TWENTY-THIRD YEAR OF JUBILEE.
320-204 B.C.	THE PTOLEMY DYNASTY RULES EGYPT AND PALESTINE.
312-65 B.C.	THE SELEUCID DYNASTY RULES SYRIA.
312-280 B.C.	SELEUCUS I (NICATOR) RULES SYRIA.
300 B.C.	THE BEGINNING OF THE MAYA EMPIRE IN MEXICO.
285-246 B.C.	PTOLEMY II (PHILADELPHIA) RULES EGYPT. (Daniel 11:6)
285 B.C.	A PTOLEMY ORDERS THE SEPTUAGINT TRANSLATED. (This documents that the whole Old Testament pre-dates the New Testament fulfillment of the prophesies about the Messiah in Jesus).
274-232 B.C.	RAJA ASHOKA BECOMES A SUPPORTING MEMBER OF THE BUDDHIST FAITH AND COMMISSIONS AN EVANGELISTIC OUT REACH TO TIBET, CHINA, AND SOUTHEAST ASIA. THE TEACHINGS OF BUDDHA ARE PUT INTO WRITTEN FORM FOR THE FIRST TIME. THEY ARE THEN LOST AT SEA, RESCUED AND RESTORED. AFTER RESTORATION THE MANUSCRIPTS READ THAT THE GREAT SAVIOR WILL COME IN 5,000 YEARS INSTEAD OF 500 YEARS. HOWEVER THEY STILL TEACH THAT THE BUDDHIST FAITH IS TO LAST ONLY 500 YEARS.
271 B.C.	TWENTY FOURTH YEAR OF JUBILEE.
261-246 B.C.	ANTIOCHUS II (THEOS) RULES SYRIA.
246-221 B.C.	PTOLEMY III (EUERGETES I) RULES EGYPT. (Daniel 11:7, 8)
246-226 B.C.	SELEUCUS II (CALLINICUS) RULES SYRIA. (Daniel 11:9)
242 B.C.	THE ROMANS DEFEAT THE CARTHAGINIANS AT SEA ENDING THE 1ST PUNIC WAR.

226-223 B.C.	SELEUCUS III (CERAUNUS) RULES SYRIA (Daniel 11:9).
223-187 B.C.	ANTIOCHUS III (THE GREAT) RULES SYRIA (Daniel 11:10-18).
221 B.C.	TWENTY-FIFTH YEAR OF JUBILEE.
221-204 B.C.	PTOLEMY IV (PHILOPATER) RULES EGYPT (Daniel 11: 11, 12, 14).
218 B.C.	ANTIOCHUS III DEFEATS PTOLEMY AT MOUNT TABOR NEAR MEGIDDO.
204-165 B.C.	THE SELEUCIDS RULE SYRIA AND PALESTINE.
201 B.C.	HANNIBAL DEFEATED BY THE ROMANS ENDING THE SECOND PUNIC WAR.
187-175 B.C.	SELEUCUS IV (PHILOPATOR) RULES SYRIA (Daniel 11: 20).
181-145 B.C.	PTOLEMY VI (PHILOMETOR) RULES EGYPT.
175-164 B.C.	ANTIOCHUS IV (EPIPHANES) RULES SYRIA (Daniel 11:21-35).
171 B.C.	TWENTY-SIXTH YEAR OF JUBILEE.
171 B.C.	ANTIOCHUS EPIPHANES SENDS ORDERS TO JERUSALEM AND THE CITIES OF JUDAH THAT THEY SHOULD NOT FOLLOW THE LAW OF MOSES. HE FORBIDS WHOLE BURNT OFFERINGS, SACRIFICES, AND DRINK OFFERINGS IN THE SANCTUARY. THE SABBATHS AND FEASTS ARE TO BE IGNORED AND THE SANCTUARY AND PRIESTS ARE TO DO THINGS THAT WOULD CAUSE THEM TO BE CONSIDERED POLLUTED (1 Macc. 1).
168 B.C.	MACCABEAN (HASMONEAN) REVOLT AGAINST ANTIOCHUS, A SELEUCID KING, BEGINS.
168 B.C.	MACEDONIA IS CONQUERED BY ROME. IT IS DIVIDED INTO FOUR SELF-GOVERNING REGIONS PAYING TRIBUTE TO ROME.
165 B.C.	THE JERUSALEM TEMPLE IS CLEANSED AND REDEDICATED.

165-163 B.C.	HASMONEAN KINGS RULE JUDAH.
165-142 B.C.	THREE MACCABEAN BROTHERS (JOHNATHAN, JUDAS, AND SIMON) LEAD THE FIGHT FOR JUDEAN INDEPENDENCE. JOHNATHAN SERVES AS HIGH PRIEST, JUDAH LEADS THE ARMY. JUDAH DIES AND SIMON TAKES OVER HIS ROLE, JOHNATHAN DIES AND SIMON TAKES OVER HIS ROLE, BECOMING A HIGH PRIEST-KING. SOME CHALLENGE THE CONCEPT OF MACCABEAN HIGH PRIESTS OF THE WRONG LINEAGE FOR HIGH PRIESTS.
164-162 B.C.	ANTIOCHUS V (EUPATOR) RULES SYRIA.
162-150 B.C.	DEMETRIUS I (SOTER) RULES SYRIA.
150-145 B.C.	ALXANDER BALAS RULES SYRIA.
148-146 B.C.	A MACEDONIAN REVOLT IS PUT DOWN AND IT BECOMES A ROMAN PROVINCE.
149-146 B.C.	THIRD PUNIC WAR ENDS WITH THE DESTRUCTION OF CARTHAGE.
142-135 B.C.	SIMON RULES PALESTINE AS A HIGH PRIEST-KING.
135 B.C.	MATHIAS CURTIS, THE GREAT GRAND FATHER OF JOSEPHUS, IS BORN TO THE DAUGHTER OF JOHNATHAN, THE ORIGINAL MACCABEAN HIGH PRIEST.
135-104 B.C.	JOHN HYRCANUS, SIMON'S SON, BECOMES A HIGH PRIEST-KING OF PALESTINE. THE QUMRAN COMMUNITY DOES ITS FIRST BUILDING.
133 B.C.	SPAIN AND PERGAMUS COME UNDER ROMAN RULE.
121 B.C.	TWENTY-SEVENTH YEAR OF JUBILEE.
109 B.C.	ARMENIA MAJOR BECOMES A ROMAN PROVINCE.
104-103B.C.	ARISTOBULUS, SON OF JOHN HYRCANUS, BECOMES HIGH PRIEST-KING OF PALESTINE. QUMRAN BECOMES OCCUPIED.

103-76 B.C.	ALEXANDER JANNACUS, SON OF ARISTOBULUS, BECOMES HIGH PRIEST-KING OF PALESTINE. HE PLUNDERS SECTS OF JEWS WHO OBJECT TO HIS DUAL ROLE (THIS INCLUDES THAT OF QUMRAN). JULIUS CAESAR IS BORN (7/12). SOME OF THE DEAD SEA SCROLLS ARE WRITTEN.
76-67 B.C.	SALOME ALEXANDRA, WIFE OF ALEXANDER JANNAEUS, RULES PALESTINE. SHE FAVORS FUNDAMENTALISTS. PHARISEES SHARE HER POWER. HYRCANUS II IS HIGH PRIEST.
75 B.C.	BITHYNIA COMES UNDER ROMAN RULE.
71 B.C.	TWENTY-EIGHTH YEAR OF JUBILEE.
67 B.C.	JOSEPH, THE GRAND FATHER OF JOSEPHUS, IS BORN.
67-63 B.C.	CIVIL WAR IN PALESTINE BETWEEN JOHN HYRCANUS II AND ARISTOBULUS II, BOTH SONS OF SALOME. BOTH APPEALED TO POMPEY (ROME) FOR HELP. ROME SUPPORTS JOHN. ARISTOBULUS DECLARES HIMSELF HIGH PRIEST-KING AND DEFEATS JOHN IN BATTLE.
63 B.C.	POMPEY TAKES JERUSALEM, REINSTATES JOHN AS HIGH PRIEST, BUT MAKES AN IDUMEAN (EDOMITE), ANTIPATHER (HEROD THE GREAT'S FATHER) KING.
57 B.C.	GAUL BECOMES A ROMAN PROVINCE.
55 B.C.	GABINIUS DEFEATS ALEXANDER AT MOUNT TABOR NEAR MEGGIDO.
50-48 B.C.	CIVIL WAR BETWEEN JULIUS CAESAR AND POMPEY ENDS IN THE DEATH OF POMPEY.
44 B.C.	JULIUS CAESAR KILLED IN THE ROMAN SENATE ON MARCH 15TH BY BRUTUS, CASSIUS AND MARK ANTHONY.

43 B.C.	CONSULS HIRTIUS AND PANSA JOIN WITH OCTAVIAN DEFEAT ANTONY AT MODENA. THE CONSULS ARE SLAIN IN THE CONFLICT, BUT ANTONY IS BEATEN AND RETREATS ACROSS THE ALPS WHERE HE JOINED LEPIDUS. OCTAVIUS THEN JOINED ANTHONY AND LEPIDUS TO FORCE ROME TO RECOGNIZE THEM AS A RULING TRIUMVIRATE.
42 B.C.	OCTAVIUS CAESAR AND ANTHONY DEFEAT BRUTUS AND CASSIUS AT PHILIPPI.
40-37 B.C.	PARTHIA INVADES PALESTINE. ANTIGONUS, SON OF ARISTOBULUS, BECOMES HIGH PRIEST-KING IN JERUSALEM AS A PARTHIAN PUPPET.
37 B.C.	HEROD THE GREAT PLACED ON THE JEWISH THROWN AFTER HE RETAKES JERUSALEM FOR ROME. HE FAVORS THE ESSENES (QUMRAN SECT) BECAUSE THEY PREDICT HIS VICTORY. SEXTUS POMPEY IS SLAIN...
35 B.C.	THE ROMAN EMPIRE IS DIVIDED BETWEEN OCTAVIAN (WEST) AND ANTONY (EAST).
31 B.C.	OCTAVIUS DEFEATS MARK ANTHONY IN A NAVAL BATTLE AT ACTIUM. AN EARTH QUAKE IN THE JERUSALEM AREA KILLS 30,000. QUMRAN BECOMES UNOCCUPIED.
30 B.C.	MARK ANTHONY AND CLEOPATRA DIE (THE LAST OF THE PTOLEMIES). EGYPT BECOMES A ROMAN PROVINCE.

CHAPTER SIX
A CHRISTIAN CHRONOLOGY OF HISTORY
(27 B.C. – 96 A.D.)
A TIME LINE OF HUMAN HISTORY
FROM A CHRISTIAN PROSPECTIVE
Compiled by "God's Friend"

27 B.C.-14 A.D	OCTAVIUS IS GIVEN THE TITLE, "AUGUSTUS." HE RULES AS THE FIRST ROMAN EMPEROR.
21 B.C.	TWENTY-NINTH YEAR OF JUBILEE
20 B.C.	BIRTH OF PHILO, ALEXANDRIAN JEWISH PHILOSOPHER.
7-1 B.C.	BIRTH OF JOHN THE BAPTIST AND JESUS, DEATH OF THE BABIES AROUND BETHLEHEM. JESUS WAS BORN OF A VIRGIN IN BETHLEHEM. HE WAS OF THE LINEAGE OF SHEM, ABRAHAM, ISAAC, JACOB, JUDAH, JESSE, AND DAVID. JOSEPH TAKES JESUS TO EGYPT AFTER BEING WARNED BY AN ANGEL OF HEROD'S COMING ATTEMPT TO KILL JESUS. AFTER HEROD'S DEATH THE CHILD IS BROUGHT OUT OF EGYPT AND RAISED IN NAZARETH (FROM A ROUTE WORD THAT MEANS "BRANCH").
5 B.C.	BIRTH OF JESUS (Luke 3:23, Daniel 9:24-27; 12:1-13) (Birth on 15TH of Ethanim 5 B.C. – 1ST day of Feast of Tabernacles; about Oct. 7th, 5 B.C. He was circumcised on the last day of the Feast of Tabernacles. SEE Luke 2:21-38)

Late 4 B.C.	MAGI (MEDES FROM THE MOUNTAINS OF INDIA, NORTH OF NEPAL) VISIT HEROD LOOKING FOR THE NEWLY BORN MESSIAH. HEROD KILLS THE BABY BOYS AROUND BETHLEHEM. (Matthew 2: 1-18).
4-3 B.C.	HEROD THE GREAT DIES AND HEROD ANTIPAS RULES AS TETRARCH OF GALILEE AND PERAEA.
3 B.C.-6 A.D.	HEROD ARCHELAUS RULES JUDEA. AN ANGEL APPEARS TO JOSEPH AND CALLS HIS FAMILY OUT OF EGYPT WHERE THEY WERE SENT TO PROTECT JESUS FROM HEROD THE GREAT (Matthew 2:13-23).
3 B.C.	JOSEPH AND MARY TAKE JESUS TO BE RAISED IN NAZARETH (THE CITY OF THE BRANCH). (SEE Matthew 2:23; Luke 2:39; Zechariah3:8; 6:12; Jeremiah 23:5; 33:15; Isaiah 11:1)
1 B.C.	QUMRAN REPAIRED AND REOCCUPIED.
3-9 A.D.	BIRTH OF MATTHIAS, FATHER OF JOSEPHUS.
11 A.D.	TIBERIUS CAESAR BEGINS RULING AS CO- REGENT WITH AUGUSTUS. HE BECOMES SOLE ROMAN EMPEROR ON AUGUST 19, 14 A.D. WHEN AUGUSTUS DIES. HE HIMSELF DIES ON 3/16/37
14-37 A.D.	TIBERIUS RULES AS ROMAN EMPEROR.
23 A.D.	BIRTH OF PLINY THE ELDER, UNCLE OF AND ADOPTIVE FATHER TO PLINY THE YOUNGER.
25 A.D.	JOHN THE BAPTIST BEGINS PREACHING THE BAPTISM OF REPENTANCE FOR THE REMISSION OF SINS. HE SAYS THE ONE THAT COMES AFTER HIM IS SO HIGH THAT JOHN IS NOT EVEN WORTHY TO CARRY HIS SHOES, THAT HE WILL BAPTIZE WITH FIRE AND THE HOLY

SPIRIT (SEE 29 A.D.). JOHN IS THEN ARRESTED AND BEHEADED BY HEROD ANTIPAS.

25-29 A.D.   JESUS IS BAPTIZED AND BEGINS TEACHING AS THE FEAST OF TABERNACLES BEGINS AND AS HE TURNS 30 YEARS OLD, THE AGE FOR PRIEST TO BEGIN DIVINE SERVICE (Numbers 4; Luke 3:1, 21-23; Psalms 110:4; Hebrews 5:5,6). (In respect to the genealogies of Matthew and Luke note "Ecclesiastic History" Book 1, Chapter 7). HE SAYS THAT HE CAME NOT TO JUDGE THE WORLD BUT TO SAVE IT, BUT THAT THE WORDS HE SPEAKS WILL JUDGE THE WORLD.

JESUS DOES MUCH OF HIS TEACHING IN ZEBULUN AND NAPHTALI BY THE SEA IN THE LAND BEYOND THE JORDAN, GALILEE OF THE NATIONS. HE HEALS THE SICK DOING MANY MIRACLES. A WEEK BEFORE HIS DEATH HE RIDES INTO JERUSALEM ON A COLT THE FOAL OF AN ASS, AND THE MULTITUDES RUN BEFORE HIM SPREADING THEIR GARMENTS AND TREE BRANCHES IN HIS PATH, SAYING, "HOSANNA TO THE SON OF DAVID, BLESSED IS HE THAT COMES IN THE NAME OF THE LORD, HOSANNA IN THE HIGHEST."

JESUS TEACHES THAT THE JEWS WILL KILL HIM, BUT THAT HE WILL RETURN FROM THE GRAVE IN THREE DAYS. JESUS FURTHER WARNS THAT AFTER HIS DEATH, DURING THE LIVES OF SOME HEARING HIM, JERUSALEM AND HEROD'S TEMPLE WILL BE DESTROYED. WHEN HIS FOLLOWERS SEE THE ROMAN EAGLES GATHER OUTSIDE OF THE CITY THEY SHOULD RUN FOR THEIR LIVES.

(SEE 70 A.D.) HE WAS THEN ARRESTED
AND TRIED IN A WAY THAT BROKE MANY
OF THE LAWS OF MOSES. HE WAS LED
LIKE A LAMB TO THE SLAUGHTER. PILOT
DECLARED HIM INNOCENT SEVERAL
TIMES, BUT THE PEOPLE CRIED FOR HIS
BLOOD AND ASKED FOR ANY BLOOD
GUILT TO BE PLACED ON THEM AND
THEIR CHILDREN. HE WAS TAKEN,
BEATEN, AND HIS FOREHEAD BECOMES
SCARED. HE WAS THEN CRUCIFIED, NAILS
WERE DRIVEN THROUGH HIS HANDS
AND HIS FEET AND THE GUARDS AT
THE FOOT OF THE CROSS DIVIDED
HIS GARMENTS AND CAST LOTS FOR
HIS VESTURE. TWO THIEVES WERE
CRUCIFIED WITH HIM. BEFORE HE
WAS TAKEN DOWN FROM THE CROSS
A ROMAN SOLDIER RAN A SPEAR
THROUGH HIS SIDE TO MAKE SURE HE
WAS DEAD.
AFTER HIS DEATH A RICH MAN
PETITIONED FOR HIS BODY AND HE WAS
LAID IN A NEW TOMB. BECAUSE OF HIS
PROPHESY THAT HE WOULD LEAVE THE
GRAVE WITHIN THREE DAYS, THE TOMB
WAS SEALED AND A GUARD WAS POSTED
TO SECURE HIS BODY. ON THE THIRD
DAY THE SEAL WAS BROKEN, THE STONE
ROLLED BACK AND HE WALKED OUT
OF THE TOMB. THE GUARDS COULD
DO NOTHING. NO ONE WAS INJURED,
BUT HIS BODY WAS GONE. HE THEN
APPEARED TO OVER 500 PEOPLE WHO
KNEW HIM. HE GAVE HIS DISCIPLES,
THOSE WHO KNEW HIM BEST,
OPPORTUNITY TO ASSURE THEMSELVES
THAT HE HAD REALLY RISEN FROM THE
DEAD.

THEY ASSURED THEMSELVES TO THE
POINT THAT EVERY ONE OF THEM WAS
WILLING TO DIE AND HAVE THEIR
FAMILIES TORTURED RATHER THAN
DENY THE RESURRECTION.

29 A.D.   ON PENTECOST, FORTY-FIVE DAYS AFTER
JESUS' DEATH, THE CHURCH BEGINS
IN JERUSALEM. JESUS BAPTIZES THE
APOSTLES WITH THE HOLY SPIRIT FROM
HEAVEN AND THEY BEGIN SPEAKING
IN TONGUES (FOREIGN LANGUAGES).
PEOPLE FROM ALL DIFFERENT REGIONS
HEAR THEM TEACHING IN THEIR
NATIVE LANGUAGES. (Daniel 12: 1, 2, 7,
10-12; Matthew 27:50-54; Mark 15:38; Luke
23:44-47)

29 A.D.   THIRTIETH YEAR OF JUBILEE. (Jesus'
ministry lasts 3 ½ years, or 1290 days (28
A.D. is a Sabbath year with an added month).
He begins on the first day of the Feast of
Tabernacles as he turns 30 years old (the 15th of
Ethanim (Tishri) 25 A.D.). He dies on the 15th
of Abib (Nisan) 29 A.D.).

32-33 A.D.   MARTYRDOM OF STEVEN, CONVERSION
OF PAUL, SPREAD OF THE CHURCH
THROUGH OUT PALESTINE, SYRIA, AND
SAMARIA.

36-70 A.D.   THOMAS PREACHES TO THE PARTHIANS,
MEDES, PERSIANS, CARMANIANS,
HYRCANIANS, BACTRIANS, MAGIANS,
AND IS KILLED FOR THE GOSPEL IN
CALAMINA, INDIA.
SIMON ZELOTES PREACHES THE
GOSPEL IN MAURITANIA, AFRICA, AND
BRITAIN BEFORE BEING CRUCIFIED FOR
THE GOSPEL.
BARTHOLOMEW CARRIES THE
GOSPEL TO INDIA AND TRANSLATES
THE GOSPEL OF MATTHEW INTO THEIR

	LANGUAGE. HE THEN PREACHES IN ARMENIA WHERE HE IS CRUCIFIED.
37 A.D.	BIRTH OF JOSEPHUS.
37-41 A.D.	CALIGULA (CAIUS CAESAR GERMANICUS) RULES IN ROME.
37 A.D.	HEROD AGRIPPA I BECOMES KING OF GAULONITIS, TRACHONITIS, AND PANEAS.
37-60 A.D.	MATTHEW WRITES HIS GOSPEL. HE SAID JESUS TAUGHT THAT THE REAL GOD IS NOT GOD OF THE DEAD, BUT OF THE LIVING. HE RECORDS THAT JESUS TOLD HIS FOLLOWERS TO CORRECT ERRANT BROTHERS THROUGH VERBAL AND SOCIAL PERSUASION AND NOT THROUGH PHYSICAL OR SECULAR COERCION. VENGEANCE IS RESERVED FOR GOD. JESUS ALSO TAUGHT THAT THE RELIGIOUS TITLE OF "FATHER" WAS TO BE RESERVED FOR GOD ONLY.
39 A.D.	HEROD AGRIPPA I RECEIVES THE ADDITIONAL TERRITORIES, GALILEE AND PERAEA.
40 A.D.	HEROD AGRIPPA I RECEIVES ADDITIONAL TERRITORIES OF JUDEA AND SAMARIA.
41-54 A.D.	CLAUDIUS CAESAR RULES IN ROME AFTER KILLING CAIUS.
43 A.D.	JAMES THE BROTHER OF JOHN KILLED BY HEROD AGRIPPA I.
44 A.D.	HEROD AGRIPPA I KILLED BY GOD.
47 A.D.	PAUL BEGINS HIS FIRST MISSIONARY JOURNEY.
49 A.D.	THE JERUSALEM COUNCIL DISCUSSES WHAT SHOULD BE BOUND ON THE CHRISTIAN FROM THE LAW OF MOSES. THE HOLY SPIRIT SAYS THAT THE ONLY THINGS TO BE BOUND ON THE

	CHRISTIAN FROM THE LAW OF MOSES IS TO ABSTAIN FROM MEATS OFFERED TO IDOLS, FROM BLOOD, FROM THINGS STRANGLED, AND FROM SEXUAL IMMORALITY.
50 A.D.	PAUL BEGINS HIS SECOND MISSIONARY JOURNEY. JEWS ARE EXPELLED FROM ROME. PHILO DIES.
50-63 A.D.	JAMES THE BROTHER OF JESUS WRITES JAMES.
52-53 A.D.	PAUL WRITES 1, 2 THESSALONIANS. THE CHURCH IS WARNED OF A COMING APOSTASY IN WHICH LEADERS OF THE CHURCH WILL USURP THE AUTHORITY OF GOD (SEE 37-380, 395, 408, 1022, 1099, 1150, 1209, 1215, 1572, 1598, 1608, 1610, 1628, AND, 1640 A.D.). TO KEEP YOUR SALVATION YOU MUST HOLD TO THE APOSTLES' TEACHINGS. THE APOSTASY IS TO LAST UNTIL JESUS RETURNS. SOMEONE (PROBABLY THE SPIRIT) IS RESTRAINING THE APOSTASY THROUGH "IT" (PROBABLY THE GIFT OF MIRACULOUS KNOWLEDGE), BUT WILL GET OUT OF THE MIDDLE OF THINGS BEFORE THE APOSTASY BEGINS. DAMNATION COMES THROUGH A LACK OF LOVE OF THE TRUTH.
52-60 A.D.	ANTONIUS FELIX IS ROMAN PREFECT IN JUDEA.
53 A.D.	PAUL BEGINS HIS THIRD MISSIONARY JOURNEY.
53-56 A.D.	JOSEPHUS IN JERUSALEM STUDIES THE ESSENES, PHARISEES, AND SADDUCEES TO DETERMINE WHICH GROUP HE WANTS TO JOIN. HE CHOOSES THE PHARISEES.
54 A.D.	JEWS RETURN TO ROME AFTER CLAUDIUS' DEATH.

54-68 A.D.	NERO RULES IN ROME.
57-58 A.D.	PAUL WRITES GALATIANS, 1, 2 CORINTHIANS, ROMANS. HE PROPHESIES THAT THE HOLY SPIRIT WILL QUIT GIVING THE GIFT OF TONGUES, PROPHESY, AND MIRACULOUS KNOWLEDGE WHEN THE MATURE BODY OF CHRIST OR PERFECT THING COMES, BUT WILL CONTINUE TO GIVE THE GIFTS OF FAITH, HOPE, AND LOVE (SEE 96 A.D.). HE FURTHER TEACHES THAT THE CHRISTIANS ARE NOW THE ISRAEL OF GOD, SONS OF GOD, THE CHILDREN OF PROMISE. ALL, JEWS AND NON-JEWS, HAVE ACCESS TO THIS RELATIONSHIP THROUGH OBEDIANT FAITH IN JESUS.
60-62 A.D.	PORCIUS FESTUS IS ROMAN PREFECT IN JUDEA.
60-65? A.D.	PAUL DICTATES HEBREWS (HIS BEST SCRIBAL HELPERS ARE ABSENT AND HE HAS POOR VISIO
62 A.D.	MARK WRITES PETER'S GOSPEL. PLINY THE YOUNGER IS BORN. MARK, LUKE, AND MATTHEW ALL SAID JESUS PROPHESIED THE DESTRUCTION OF JERUSALEM IN THEIR GENERATION. THE CHRISTIANS WERE TOLD TO RUN FROM JERUSALEM WHEN THEY SEE THE EAGLES GATHER OUTSIDE THE WALLS OF JERUSALEM (SEE 68 A.D.).
62-63 A.D.	PAUL WRITES EPHESIANS, PHILIPPIANS, COLOSSIANS, AND PHILEMON WHILE HE IS A PRISONER IN ROME. LUKE WRITES PAUL'S GOSPEL AND THE BOOK OF ACTS. PAUL TEACHES THAT THE GENTILES USE TO BE ALIENATED FROM THE COMMON WEALTH OF ISRAEL, BUT NOW JESUS RECONCILES BOTH INTO ONE BODY AND THEY ARE CITIZENS WITH

	THE SAINTS AND MEMBERS OF THE HOUSEHOLD OF GOD.
63 A.D.	PAUL RELEASED FROM PRISON AND GOES TO PREACH IN SPAIN.
63-64 A.D.	JOSEPHUS IS IN ROME PLEADING WITH NERO'S WIFE FOR URGENT RELEASE OF JEWISH PRIESTS BROUGHT TO ROME IN BONDS.
63-68 A.D.	PETER WRITES 1, 2 PETER. HE PROPHESIES THAT IN THE LAST DAYS EVIL SCOFFERS WILL MAKE JEST OF CHRISTIANS ASKING, "WHEN IS JESUS COMING AGAIN?" THEY WILL SAY ALL THINGS HAVE ALWAYS PROCEDED THE SAME, FORGETTING ABOUT NOAH'S FLOOD. GOD IS PRESERVING OUR WORLD FOR DESTRUCTION BY FIRE, IS PATIENT, GIVING THEM TIME TO REPENT, NOT WANTING THEM TO PERISH (SEE 1795, 1830, 1837, 1858, 1881A.D.).
66-67 A.D.	PAUL WRITES 1TIMOTHY AND TITUS. CHRISTIAN CHURCHES ARE ORGANIZED WITH JESUS AS KING IN HEAVEN, AND EACH CONGREGATION UNDER THE LEADERSHIP OF MORAL, LOCAL, FAMILY MEN KNOWN AS BISHOPS. HE PROPHESIED THAT IN LATER TIMES SOME WILL LEAVE THE FAITH ORDERING OTHERS TO NOT MARRY AND TO ABSTAIN FROM MEAT.
66-67 A.D.	JOSEPHUS LEADS A TRANS-JORDAN ARMY OF OVER 150,000.
67 A.D.	VESPASIAN DEFEATS JEWISH FORCES AT MOUNT TABOR, NEAR MEGGIDO.
68 A.D.	PAUL WRITES 2 TIMOTHY. HE ASSERTS THAT THE INSPIRED SCRIPTURES CAN MAKE A MAN OF GOD COMPLETE, THOROUGHLY FURNISHED UNTO

	ALL GOOD WORKS. PAUL AND PETER ARE EXECUTED IN ROME. JOSEPHUS IS CAPTURED BY THE ROMANS. THE QUMRAN COMMUNITY IS ANNIHILATED BY THE ROMAN GARRISON AT JERICHO. NERO DIES.
	THE ROMANS, WHO HAD COME TO BESIEGE JERUSALEM, BRIEFLY LIFT THE SIEGE TO ESCORT VESPASIAN TO THE SEA SO HE CAN GO TO ROME WHERE HE HOPES TO BECOME EMPEROR. BECAUSE OF PROPHECY, THE CHRISTIANS FLEE JERUSALEM (SEE 62 A.D.). ESSENES CEASE TO EXIST.
68-86 A.D.	ROMANS OCCUPY THE RUINS OF QUMRAN.
69 A.D.	GALBA, OTHO, VITELLIUS, AND VESPASIAN CONTEST THE THROWN OF ROME.
69-79 A.D.	VESPASIAN RULES IN ROME.
70-74 A.D.	DESTRUCTION OF JERUSALEM WITH HORRID CONSEQUENCES FOR ANY INHABITANTS AFTER 68 A.D. ROMANS CONDUCT MOP-UP OPERATIONS THROUGHOUT JUDEA. TITUS, SON OF VESPASIAN, LEADS THE ASSAULT ON JERUSALEM. 1,100,000 JEWS DIE, NOT COUNTING THOSE IN GALILEE. 17,000 ARE SOLD INTO THE PROVINCES AS SLAVES. TWO THOUSAND ARE TAKEN TO ROME FOR TITUS' TRIUMPH AND THEN ARE SLAIN OR DEVOURED IN THE GAMES.
70-79 A.D.	THE EPISTLE OF BARNABAS IS WRITTEN, BUT NOT ACCEPTED AS INSPIRED OF GOD. IT PREDICTS THE END OF THE WORLD ABOUT SIX THOUSAND YEARS AFTER CREATION.

74 A.D.	MASADA, THE LAST JEWISH STRONGHOLD, FALLS.
79-81 A.D.	TITUS RULES AS ROMAN EMPEROR.
79 A.D.	THIRTY FIRST YEAR OF JUBILEE. DEATH OF PLINY THE ELDER AT THE ERUPTION OF MT. VESUVIUS THAT DESTROYED POMPEII. HE WAS A PROLIFIC NATURALIST AUTHOR, AND ADMIRAL OF THE ROMAN NAVY. DRUSILLA AND HER SON, AGRIPPA III, ALSO DIE IN THIS ERUPTION. DRUSILLA IS WIFE OF FELIX, DAUGHTER OF HEROD AGRIPPA I, SISTER OF HEROD AGRIPPA II.
80 A.D.	ANDREW, AFTER PREACHING TO THE SCYTHIANS AND ETHIOPIANS, IS CRUCIFIED IN ACHAIA.
81-96 A.D.	DOMITIAN RULES IN ROME.
90 A.D.	JOHN WRITES 1, 2, 3, JOHN. HE TEACHES THAT ANYONE WHO DENIES THE FATHER AND JESUS, OR SAYS THAT JESUS IS NOT THE CHRIST (ANOINTED ONE-MESSIAH) IS AN ANTICHRIST.
90-96 A.D.	PERSECUTION OF THE CHRISTIANS UNDER DOMITAIN.
95 A.D.	CLEMENT OF ROME WRITES TO THE CORINTHIAN CHURCH. HIS WRITING IS NOT ACCEPTED AS INSPIRED OF GOD.
96-97 A.D.	JOHN WRITES REVELATION AND THE GOSPEL OF JOHN. HE PROPHESIES OF A ROMAN RELIGIOUS MOTHER OF HARLOTS THAT WILL KILL THE SAINT AND FORBID THEM THE RIGHT OF COMMERCE. HER POWER IS TO LAST 1260 YEARS (SEE 380, 1640 A.D.). MOVING FROM JOHN'S TIME, HE PREDICTS CONQUEST AND PROSPERITY (SEE 98 A.D.) FOLLOWED BY WAR AND SLAUGHTER (SEE 180 A.D.), FOLLOWED BY FAMINE WITH

PROTECTION OF GRAPES AND OLIVES
(SEE 293 A.D.) FOLLOWED BY MUCH
DYING. THEN THERE WOULD BE A
FALSE EXPECTATION OF RELIEF FROM
PERSECUTION FOR THE CHRISTIAN
(SEE 315 A.D.), THEN A COLLAPSE IN
LEADERSHIP (SEE 325 A.D., 360 A.D., AND
380 A.D.). DESTRUCTION WOULD FIRST
COME BY LAND (SEE 378, 403, 408, AND
410 A.D.), THEN BY THE SEA (SEE 429,
439, AND 455 A.D.), THEN DOWN THE
RIVER VALLEYS (SEE 450, 452, AND 453
A.D.). THIS WOULD BE FOLLOWED BY
ANOTHER COLLAPSE IN LEADERSHIP
(SEE 476 A.D.). THERE WOULD THEN
COME TORMENT FROM THOSE LEAD
BY THE KING OF THE DEAD FOR ONE
HUNDRED AND FIFTY YEARS (SEE 612
A.D. AND 762 A.D.). DURING THIS TIME
PLANT LIFE WOULD BE PROTECTED (SEE
632 A.D.).
THEN THERE WOULD BE A SECOND
WAVE OF TORMENT FROM THOSE LEAD
BY THE KING OF THE DEAD FROM
ACROSS THE EUPHRATES RIVER. THIS
WOULD LAST FOR 391 YEARS (SEE 1062
AND 1453 A.D.). THEIR NUMBER WOULD
BE EXTREMELY LARGE. THEY WOULD
USE FIRE AND BRIMSTONE IN THEIR
WEAPONS.
THEN A BOOK, SWEET AT FIRST, BUT
WITH SOME BITTER AFTER EFFECTS,
WILL BE USED AND THE TEACHINGS
WILL GO BEFORE MANY NATIONS
(SEE 1455, 1530, 1615, 1804-1830 A.D.) THE
TEACHING WILL BE STOPPED FOR A
SHORT TIME (31/2 DAYS OR YEARS-PROBABLY
YEARS)(SEE 1572, 1608, 1610 , 1861-1865 A.D.).
KINGDOMS WILL SUBMIT TO GOD.
THIS WILL MAKE THE NATIONS ANGRY

(THOSE ALLIED WITH RUSSIA AND MONGOLIA). AND THEY WILL SURROUND THE CAMPS OF THE SAINTS AND TRY TO DESTROY GOD'S PEOPLE (SEE 597 B.C. AND 1279, 1917, 1932, 1947, 1959, 1974, 1984, 1986, AND 1996-PRESENT A.D.). GOD WILL DESTROY THEM (SEE 597-587 B.C. EZE. 38, 39). THEN WILL COME THE FINAL JUDGMENT AND HEAVEN. JOHN WARNS THAT ANYONE THAT ADDS TO THE BOOK OF PROPHESY WILL RECEIVE THE PLAGUES OF THE BOOK.

96-98 A.D.   NERVA RULES THE ROMAN EMPIRE.

98-100 A.D.   THE DEATH OF JOHN, THE LAST LIVING APOSTLE.

CHAPTER SEVEN
A CHRISTIAN CHRONOLOGY OF HISTORY
(96 A.D. – 476 A.D.)
A TIME LINE OF HUMAN HISTORY
FROM A CHRISTIAN PROSPECTIVE
Compiled by "God's Friend"

98-117 A.D.	TRAJAN RULES IN ROME. HE IS FROM CRETE, AN AREA RENOWNED FOR ARCHERS. HE EXPANDS THE EMPIRE OVER THE NATIONS OF THE EAST FROM THE MOUNTAINS OF ARMENIA TO THE PERSIAN GULF.
98-180 A.D.	EMPERORS ARE SELECTED FOR MERIT, NOT LINEAGE. THIS IS A TIME OF EXPANSION, PROSPERITY, AND UNITY.
100 A.D.	JOSEPHUS AND THE APOSTLE JOHN DIE. (JOHN IS THE LAST OF THE APOSTLES).
110-115 A.D.	LETTER OF IGNATIUS
113 A.D.	PLINY THE YOUNGER, GOVERNOR OF BYTHYNIA, DIES.
115 A.D.	IGNATIUS OF ANTIOCH MARTYRED AND THROWN TO LIONS AT ROME.
117-138 A.D.	HADRIAN RULES IN ROME.
129 A.D.	THIRTY SECOND YEAR OF JUBILEE.
132 A.D.	HADRIAN BUILDS A TEMPLE TO JUPITER IN JERUSALEM.
132-135 A.D.	THE SECOND JEWISH REVOLT TAKES PLACE. JEWISH REBELS OCCUPY QUMRAN. QUMRAN LEFT DESERTED FROM 135 A.D. TO THE PRESENT.

136 A.D.	HADRIAN ESTABLISHES A HEATHEN TEMPLE AND REBUILDS JERUSALEM AS A PAGAN CITY WHICH IS RENAMED "AELIA CAPITOLINA" AND WHICH THE JEWS ARE FORBIDDEN TO ENTER.
138-161 A.D.	ANTONINUS PIUS RULES AS ROMAN EMPEROR.
155-156 A.D.	POLYCARP, A STUDENT OF THE APOSTLE JOHN, AN ELDER TO THE CHURCH AT SMYRNA IS MARTYRED.
161-180 A.D.	MARCUS AURELIUS RULES AS ROMAN EMPEROR.
179 A.D.	THIRTY-THIRD YEAR OF JUBILEE.
180-285 A.D.	OVER FIFTY EMPERORS AND TWENTY PRETENDERS ASCEND THE THROWN OF ROME. VERY FEW DIE A NATURAL DEATH. THIS IS A PERIOD OF CONSTANT CIVIL STRIFE FROM JEALOUSY, PERSONAL AMBITION, AND GREED.
180-192 A.D.	COMMODUS RULES AS ROMAN EMPEROR.
192-193 A.D.	PERTINAX RULES AS ROMAN EMPEROR.
193 A.D.	DIDIUS JULIANUS RULES AS ROMAN EMPEROR.
193-211 A.D.	SEPTIMUS SEVERUS RULES AS ROMAN EMPEROR.
193-194 A.D.	PESCENNIUS NIGER RULES AS ROMAN EMPEROR.
193-197 A.D.	CLODIUS ALBINUS RULES AS ROMAN EMPEROR.
211-217 A.D.	ANTONINUS (CARACALLA) RULES AS ROMAN EMPEROR.
211 A.D.	GETA RULES AS ROMAN EMPEROR.
217-218 A.D.	MARCRINUS RULES AS ROMAN EMPEROR.
218 A.D.	DIADUMENIANUS RULES AS ROMAN EMPEROR.

218-222 A.D.	ELAGABALUS, SELEUCUS, URANIUS, GELLIUS MAXIMUS AND VERUS RULE AS ROMAN EMPERORS.
222-225 A.D.	SEVERUS ALEXANDER AND TAURINUS RULE AS ROMAN EMPERORS.
225-227 A.D.	L. SEIUS SALLUSTIUS RULES AS ROMAN EMPEROR.
229 A.D.	THIRTY-FOURTH YEAR OF JUBILEE.
235-238 A.D.	MAXIMINUS THRAX, MAGNUS, AND QUARTINUS RULES AS ROMAN EMPERORS.
238 A.D.	GORIAN I, GORIAN II, PUPIENUS (MAXIMUS), AND BALBINUS RULE AS ROMAN EMPERORS.
238-244-A.D.	GORDIAN III RULES AS ROMAN EMPEROR.
240 A.D.	SABINIANUS RULES AS ROMAN EMPEROR.
244-249 A.D.	PHILIP THE ARAB, SILBANNACUS, AND SPONSIANUS RULE AS ROMAN EMPERORS.
248 A.D.	PACATIANUS AND IOTAPIANUS RULE AS ROMAN EMPERORS.
247-249 A.D.	PHILIP IUNIOR RULES AS ROMAN EMPEROR.
250 A.D.	L. PRISCUS AND IULIUS VALENS LICINIANUS RULE AS ROMAN EMPERORS.
251-253 A.D.	TREBONIUS GALLUS AND VOLUSIANUS RULE AS ROMAN EMPERORS.
253 A.D.	URANIUS ANTONINUS AND AEMILIUS AEMILIANUS RULE AS ROMAN EMPERORS.
253-260 A.D.	VALERIAN AND MAREADES RULE AS ROMAN EMPERORS.
253-268 A.D.	GALLIENUS, CELSUS, AND SATUENINUS RULE AS ROMAN EMPERORS.
260 A.D.	INGENUUS AND REGALIANUS RULE AS ROMAN EMPERORS.

260-261 A.D.	MACRIANUS SENIOR, MACRIANUS IUNIOR, AND QUIETUS RULE AS ROMAN EMPERORS.
260-269 A.D.	POSTUMUS, A GALLIC EMPEROR, RULES.
261 A.D.	PISO, VALENS, BALLISTA, AND MUSSIUS AEMILIANUS RULE AS ROMAN EMPERORS.
262 A.D.	MEMOR RULES AS ROMAN EMPEROR.
262-268 A.D.	AUREOLUS RULES AS ROMAN EMPEROR.
268-270 A.D.	CLAUDIUS II, GOTHICUS, AND CENSORINUS RULE AS ROMAN EMPERORS.
269- A.D.	LAELIANUS AND MARIUS, GALLIC EMPERORS, RULE.
269-270 A.D.	VICTORINUS, A GALLIC EMPEROR, RULES.
270 A.D.	QUINTILLUS RULES AS ROMAN EMPEROR.
270-275 A.D.	AURELIAN RULES AS ROMAN EMPEROR.
270-271 A.D.	FELICISSIMUS RULES AS ROMAN EMPEROR.
271-272 A.D.	DOMITIANUS, URBANUS, AND SEPTIMIUS RULE AS ROMAN EMPERORS.
271-274 A.D.	TETRICUS I, A GALLIC EMPEROR, RULES.
272 A.D.	VABALLATHUS RULES AS ROMAN EMPEROR.
273 A.D.	FIRMUS RULES AS ROMAN EMPEROR.
273 A.D.	FAUSTINUS, A GALLIC EMPEROR, RULES.
273-274 A.D.	TETRICUS II, A GALLIC EMPEROR, RULES.
275-276 A.D.	TACITUS RULES AS ROMAN EMPEROR.
276 A.D.	FLORIANUS RULES AS ROMAN EMPEROR.
276-282 A.D.	PROBUS RULES AS ROMAN EMPEROR.
279 A.D.	THIRTY-FIFTH YEAR OF JUBILEE.
280 A.D.	BONOSUS RULES AS ROMAN EMPEROR.
280-281 A.D.	PROCULUS RULES AS ROMAN EMPEROR.
281 A.D.	SATURNINUS RULES AS ROMAN EMPEROR.
282-283 A.D.	CARUS RULES AS ROMAN EMPEROR.

283-284 A.D.	NUMERIANUS RULES AS ROMAN EMPEROR.
283-285 A.D.	CARINUS RULES AS ROMAN EMPEROR.
284-305 A.D.	DIOCLETIAN RULES AS ROMAN EMPEROR.
285-310? A.D.	MAXIMIANUS HERCULIUS AND IULIANUS RULE AS ROMAN EMPERORS.
285-286 A.D.	AMANDUS AND AELIANUS RULE AS ROMAN EMPERORS.
286-293 A.D.	CARAUSIUS, A BRITISH EMPEROR, RULES.
293-297 A.D.	ALLECTUS, A BRITISH EMPEROR, RULES.
293-296 A.D.	CONSTANTIUS I CHLORUS RULES AS ROMAN EMPEROR.
293-311 A.D.	GALERIUS RULES AS ROMAN EMPEROR. A VERY STRICT, RIGOROUS INQUISITION INTO THE OWNERSHIP OF PROPERTY IS UNDERTAKEN FOR TAXATION PURPOSES. TORTURE IS FREELY EMPLOYED TO OBTAIN CONFESSION OF ADDITIONAL WEALTH. A LAW IS ENACTED THAT SAYS, "IF ANYONE SHALL RELIGIOUSLY CUT A VINE, OR STINT THE FRUIT OF PROLIFIC BOUGHS, AND CRAFTILY FEIGN POVERTY IN ORDER TO AVOID A FAIR ASSESSMENT, HE SHALL, IMMEDIATELY, ON DETECTION, SUFFER DEATH, AND HIS PROPERTY BE CONFISCATED."
297 A.D.	L. DOMITIUS DOMITIANUS RULES AS ROMAN EMPEROR.
297-298 A.D.	AURELIUS ACHILLEUS RULES AS ROMAN EMPEROR.
303 A.D.	EUGENIUS RULES AS ROMAN EMPEROR.
305-313 A.D.	MAXIMINUS DAIA RULES AS ROMAN EMPEROR.
305-307 A.D.	SEVERUS II RULES AS ROMAN EMPEROR.
306-312 A.D.	MAXENTIUS RULES AS ROMAN EMPEROR.
306-337 A.D.	CONSTANTINE I IS EMPEROR OF ROME.

308-309 A.D.	L. DOMITIUS ALEXANDER RULES AS ROMAN EMPEROR.
311 A.D.	WITH THE BACKING OF A ROMAN BISHOP, A BISHOP IS CHOSEN IN CARTHAGE THAT HAD LEFT THE CHURCH DURING THE DIOCLETIAN PERSECUTIONS. THERE WAS A SPLIT IN WHICH MANY CARTHAGIANS OPPOSED ANY ROMAN INTERFERENCE IN THEIR CHURCH. THE ANTI-ROME MOVEMENT SPREAD THROUGHOUT NORTH AFRICA AND REMAINED UNTIL THE ARAB CONQUEST (SEE 670-732 A.D.). AT ITS HEIGHT THIS MOVEMENT HAD OVER 270 BISHOPS.
312 A.D.	CONSTANTINE BECOMES A CHRISTIAN.
314 A.D.	VALENS RULES AS ROMAN EMPEROR.
315 A.D.	CONSTANTINE ORDERS A STOP TO THE PERSECUTION OF CHRISTIANS, AND COMMISSIONS A CHRISTIAN HISTORY BY EUSEBIUS.
324 A.D.	MARTINIANUS RULES AS ROMAN EMPEROR.
325 A.D.	CONSTANTINE LAYS THE GROUND WORK FOR A CHRISTIAN STATE CULT THAT EVOLVES INTO THE MODERN CATHOLIC CHURCH.
329 A.D.	THIRTY-SIXTH YEAR OF JUBILEE.
333-334 A.D.	CALOCAERUS RULES AS ROMAN EMPEROR.
337-340 A.D.	CONSTANTINE II RULES AS ROMAN EMPEROR.
337-350 A.D.	CONSTANTS I RULES AS ROMAN EMPEROR.
337-361 A.D.	CONSTANTIUS II RULES AS ROMAN EMPEROR.
350 A.D.	NEPOTIAN AND VETRANIO RULE AS ROMAN EMPERORS.

350-353 A.D.	MAGNENTIUS RULES AS ROMAN EMPEROR.
355 A.D.	SILVANUS RULES AS ROMAN EMPEROR.
360-363 A.D.	JULIAN RULES AS ROMAN EMPEROR. HE TRIES TO RETURN THE EMPIRE TO PAGANISM. ONLY PAGANS ARE ELEVATED TO HIGH RANK.
363-364 A.D.	JOVIAN RULES AS ROMAN EMPEROR.
364-375 A.D.	VALENTINAN RULES AS ROMAN EMPEROR.
364-378 A.D.	VALENS RULES AS ROMAN EMPEROR.
365-366 A.D.	PROCOPIUS RULES AS ROMAN EMPEROR.
366 A.D.	MARCELLUS RULES AS ROMAN EMPEROR.
367-383 A.D.	GRATIAN RULES AS ROMAN EMPEROR.
370-376 A.D.	THE HUNS OVERRUN OSTROGOTHIC AND VISIGOTHIC TERRITORIES, DRIVING THEM INTO THE ROMAN EMPIRE.
375 A.D.	FIRMUS RULES AS ROMAN EMPEROR.
375-392 A.D.	VALENTINIAN II RULES AS ROMAN EMPEROR.
376 A.D.	THE GOTHS (VISIGOTHS) IMPLORE THE PROTECTION OF ROME AGAINST THE HORDES OF HUNS POURING OUT OF MONGOLIA INTO NORTHEASTERN EUROPE. THEY WERE PLACED IN THRACE AND MOESIA AFTER HAVING THEIR WEAPONS AND CHILDREN TAKEN FROM THEM.
376-435 A.D.	THE HUNS PILLAGE THE UPPER RIVER REGIONS OF EUROPE.
378 A.D.	THE GOTHS RAVAGE THRACE, CONQUERING BY LAND.
378-395 A.D.	THEODOSIUS I RULES AS ROMAN EMPEROR. HE RECRUITS AND TRAINS THE GOTHS AS SOLDIERS. AMONG THEM IS ALARIC.
379 A.D.	THE THIRTY-SEVENTH YEAR OF JUBILEE.

380 A.D.	THEODOSIUS I ORDERS THE ROMAN ARMIES TO DO WHATEVER THEY CAN AGAINST ANY WHO DISAGREE RELIGIOUSLY WITH BISHOP DAMASCUS OF ROME. HE ALSO MADE PAGAN WORSHIP A CRIME OF HIGH TREASON. THIS IS THE BEGINNING OF STATE DICTATED AND CONTROLLED CHRISTIAN RELIGION. IT USHERS IN 1260 YEARS OF A MANDATED FORM OF CORRUPT "CHRISTIAN" STYLE RELIGIOUS PRACTICE.
383-388 A.D.	MAGNUS MAXIMUS RULES AS ROMAN EMPEROR.
384-388 A.D.	FLAVIUS VICTOR RULES AS ROMAN EMPEROR.
392-394 A.D.	EUGENIUS RULES AS ROMAN EMPEROR.
393-423 A.D.	HONORIUS RULES AS EMPEROR, AND THEN AS WESTERN EMPEROR. THE GOTHS REVOLT AND PILLAGE GREECE AND ITALY.
395 A.D.	THE ROMAN EMPIRE IS PARTITIONED INTO THE EASTERN AND WESTERN EMPIRE. THE STATE SPONSORED CHURCH IN THE WEST CONTINUES TO EVOLVE INTO THE CATHOLIC CHURCH. THE STATE SPONSORED CHURCH IN THE EAST EVOLVES INTO THE GREEK ORTHODOX CHURCH.
395-408 A.D.	ARCADIUS RULES AS EASTERN EMPEROR.
403 A.D.	THE GOTHS ARE PAID TO QUIT PILLAGING ITALY.
407 A.D.	IT IS DECLARED THAT CHRISTIANS WHO DISAGREE WITH ROMAN RELIGIOUS AUTHORITY ARE TO BE TREATED AS TRAITORS WHO REBEL AGAINST THE SECULAR AUTHORITY OF THE EMPEROR.
407-711 A.D.	CONSTANTINE III RULES AS WESTERN EMPEROR.

408 A.D.	ALERIC, LEADER OF THE GOTHS, RETURNS WITH ARMY TO ITALY AND BESIEGES ROME. AGAIN HE IS PAID OFF.
408-450 A.D.	THEODOSIUS II RULES AS EASTERN EMPEROR.
408-456 A.D.	68 LAWS DECLARING PUNISHMENT FOR CHRISTIANS WHO RESIST THE RELIGIOUS AUTHORITY OF ROME ARE ENACTED. FORCE IS USED IN FAVOR OF THE STATE CHURCH.
409 A.D.	ALARIC RETURNS AND AGAIN BESIEGES ROME. THIS TIME HE PICKS ATTALUS, A FRIEND, TO BE EMPEROR AND MAKES HIMSELF MASTER GENERAL OF ALL THE WESTERN ARMIES.
409-410 A.D.	PRISCUS ATTALUS RULES AS WESTERN EMPEROR.
409-411 A.D.	CONSTANS II AND MAXIMUS RULE AS WESTERN ROMAN EMPERORS.
410 A.D.	ALARIC BECOMES UPSET WITH ATTALUS, BESIEGES ROME, AND REMOVES HIM FROM THE THROWN. THE GOTHS TAKE ROME AND KILL AND PLUNDER FOR SIX DAYS. THEY THEN SETTLE IN SOUTHERN FRANCE.
410 A.D.	AN ALLIANCE IS MADE BETWEEN ROME AND THE HUNS. ATILLA IS SENT AS A ROMAN HOSTAGE TO INSURE THE TREATY. AISHIUS IS SENT AS A HUN HOSTAGE TO INSURE THE TREATY. EACH LEARNS THE WAYS OF THE OTHER'S CULTURE.
411-413 A.D.	JOVINUS RULES AS WESTERN EMPEROR.
412-413 A.D.	SEBASTIANUS RULES AS WESTERN EMPEROR.
421 A.D.	CONSTANTIUS III RULES AS WESTERN EMPEROR.
423-425 A.D.	JOHANNES RULES AS WESTERN EMPEROR.

425-455 A.D.	VALENTINIAN III RULES AS WESTERN EMPEROR. HE ISSUES AN EDICT COMMANDING ALL TO OBEY THE BISHOP OF ROME ON THE GROUND THAT THE LATTER HELD THE PRIMACY OF ST. PETER.
429 A.D.	THE THIRTY-EIGHTH YEAR OF JUBILEE.
429 A.D.	THE VANDALS (OSTROGOTHS), RUNNING BEFORE THE HUNS, CROSS THE PILLARS OF HERCULES (STRAITS OF GIBRALTAR) AND INVADE NORTH AFRICA (PART OF THE ROMAN EMPIRE).
435 A.D.	ATILLA BECOMES KING OF THE HUNS.
439-490 A.D.	VANDALS CONQUER CARTHAGE. THEY THEN BUILD A NAVY AND RAID THE ROMAN COASTS OF THE MEDITERRANEAN. THEY CONQUER SICILY, SACK PALERMO, AND FREQUENTLY RAID THE COAST OF LUCANIA. THEY ARE A PLAGUE BY SEA.
440-461 A.D.	LEO I AS BISHOP IN ROME DEVELOPED THE CLAIM THAT ROME, AS THE SEE OF PETER, SHOULD BE SUPREME OVER THE UNIVERSAL (CATHOLIC) CHURCH.
450 A.D.	ATILLA MASSES HIS ARMY ALONG THE RHINE AND PREPARES TO CONQUER THE ROMAN EMPIRE.
450-457 A.D.	MARCIAN RULES AS EASTERN EMPEROR.
451 A.D.	ATTILA THE HUN HAS HIS FIRST SIGNIFICNT DEFEAT AT CHALONS IN GAUL. THE OPPOSING GENERAL IS AISHIUS. THE SLAUGHTER IS MASSIVE ON BOTH SIDES (THE DEAD ARE ESTIMATED TO NUMBER 162,000 TO 300,000-ALL DYING IN A SINGLE DAY).
452 A.D.	THE CITIES OF VENETIA ARE SACKED BY THE GREATLY REDUCED HUN ARMY.
453 A.D.	ATILLA, THE MAIN HUN CHIEFTAIN, DIES. HE PLAGUED THE UPPER RIVER

	VALLEYS OF EUROPE. HIS MONGOLIAN HORDES RETREAT AND SETTLE IN THE PLAINS OF HUNGARY.
455 A.D.	PETRONIUS MAXIMUS RULES AS WESTERN EMPEROR. A VANDAL ARMY LED BY GENSERIC SACKS ROME. THEY PILLAGE ROME FOR FOURTEEN DAYS AND NIGHTS AND THEN CARRY OFF SUCH CITIZENS AS THEY DESIRE AS SLAVES.
455-456 A.D.	AVITUS RULES AS WESTERN EMPEROR.
457-461 A.D.	MAJORIAN RULES AS WESTERN EMPEROR.
457-474 A.D.	LEO I RULES AS EASTERN EMPEROR.
461-465 A.D.	LIBIUS SEVERUS RULES AS WESTERN EMPEROR.
467-472 A.D.	ANTHEMIUS RULES AS WESTERN EMPEROR.
472 A.D.	OLYBRIUS RULES AS WESTERN EMPEROR.
473-474 A.D.	GLYCERIUS RULES AS WESTERN EMPEROR.
474 A.D.	LEO II RULES AS EASTERN EMPEROR.
474-475 A.D.	JULIUS NEPOS RULES AS WESTERN EMPEROR.
474-491 A.D.	ZENO RULES AS EASTERN EMPEROR.
475-476 A.D.	ROMULUS AUGUSTULUS RULES AS WESTERN EMPEROR.
476 A.D.	THE WESTERN ROMAN EMPEROR, ROMULUS, IS DEPOSED BY ODOACER, A GERMAN CHIEF, AND THE WESTERN ROMAN EMPIRE ENDS. NO ONE WANTS TO BE THE WESTERN EMPEROR. IT IS TOO DANGEROUS A JOB.

CHAPTER EIGHT
A CHRISTIAN CHRONOLOGY OF HISTORY
(476 A.D. – 1453 A.D.)
A TIME LINE OF HUMAN HISTORY
FROM A CHRISTIAN PROSPECTIVE
Compiled by "God's Friend"

479 A.D.	THE THIRTY-NINTH YEAR OF JUBILEE.
485 A.D.	GERMANICUS WRITES THE ROMAN BISHOP (POPE) COMPLAINING THAT THE CHRISTIANS OF BRITAIN DENY ROME'S RELIGIOUS AUTHORITY AND DON'T RECOGNIZE INFANT BAPTISM BECAUSE INFANTS CAN NEITHER BELIEVE NOR REPENT (ADDITIONAL BIBLE REQUIREMENTS FOR SALVATION).
491-518 A.D.	ANASTASIUS RULES AS EASTERN EMPEROR.
518-527 A.D.	JUSTIN (JUSTINIAN DYNASTY) RULES AS EASTERN EMPEROR.
527-565 A.D.	JUSTINIAN RULES AS EASTERN EMPEROR.
529 A.D.	THE FORTIETH YEAR OF JUBILEE
565-578 A.D.	JUSTIN II RULES AS EASTERN EMPEROR.
570 A.D.	BIRTH OF MOHAMMED.
578-585 A.D.	TIBERIUS I CONSTANTINE RULES AS EASTERN EMPEROR.
582-602 A.D.	MAURICE RULES AS EASTERN EMPEROR.
596 A.D.	GREGORY, BISHOP OF ROME, ORDERED AUGUSTINE (NOT OF HIPPO) TO EVANGELIZE ENGLAND FOR THE CATHOLIC CHURCH. MUCH OF ENGLAND WAS CHRISTIAN, BUT

	NOT CATHOLIC. HE ARRIVED THERE THE NEXT YEAR WITH FORTY MONKS. CATHOLIC CENTERS OF INFLUENCE WERE ESTABLISHED AT CANTERBURY AND YORK, BUT THE CHRISTIANS ON THE WESTERN PART OF THE ISLAND BECOME ANTAGONIZED.
602-610 A.D.	PHOCAS RULES AS EASTERN EMPEROR.
601-641 A.D.	HERACLIUS RULES AS EASTERN EMPEROR.
c612 A.D.	MOHAMMED BEGINS THE RELIGION OF ISLAM.
622 A.D.	MOHAMMED IS EXILE FROM MECCA.
630 A.D.	MOHAMMED RETURNS TO MECCA.
632 A.D.	MOHAMMED DIES AND ABUBEKER LEADS THE MOSLEMS IN THE CONQUEST OF PERSIA AND SYRIA. HE ORDERS HIS SOLDIERS TO, "DESTROY NO PALM TREE, NOR BURN ANY FIELDS OF CORN. CUT DOWN NO FRUIT TREES, NOR DO ANY MISCHIEF TO CATTLE, ONLY SUCH AS YOU KILL TO EAT."
641 A.D.	HERACLONAS AND CONSTANTINE III RULE AS EASTERN EMPERORS.
641-668 A.D.	CONSTANS II RULES AS EASTERN EMPEROR.
646-647 A.D.	GREGORY RULES AS EASTERN EMPERPOR.
649-653 A.D.	OLYMPIUS RULES AS EASTERN EMPEROR.
668-685 A.D.	CONSTANTINE IV RULES AS EASTERN EMPEROR.
669 A.D.	MEZEZIUS RULES AS EASTERN EMPEROR.
670 A.D.	ARABIAN MOSLEMS INVADE THE BYZANTINE (EASTERN) EMPIRE.
670-732 A.D.	ARABS SWEEP ACROSS NORTH AFRICA AND CONQUER SPAIN.
685-695 A.D.	JUSTINIAN II RULES AS EASTERN EMPEROR (BANISHED).

c690 A.D.	CHRISTIAN CELTS ATTEMPT, WITH SOME SUCCESS, TO UNDO THE CATHOLIC INFLUENCE AROUND CANTERBURY AND YORK.
695-698 A.D.	LEONTIUS RULES AS EASTERN EMPEROR.
698-705 A.D.	TIBERIUS II RULES AS EASTERN EMPEROR.
705-711 A.D.	JUSTINIAN II RULES AS EASTERN EMPEROR (RESTORED).
711-713 A.D.	BARDANES RULES AS EASTERN EMPEROR.
713-716 A.D.	ANASTASIUS II RULES AS EASTERN EMPEROR.
716-717 A.D.	THEODOSIUS III RULES AS EASTERN EMPEROR.
717-741 A.D.	LEO III (ISAURIAN DYNASTY) RULES AS EASTERN EMPEROR.
741- A.D.	THE MOSLEM ARMIES ARE FINALLY TURNED BACK BY CHARLES MARTEL AT POITIERS IN FRANCE.
741-775 A.D.	CONSTANINE V COPRONYMUS RULES AS EASTERN EMPEROR.
742-743 A.D.	ARTABASDUS RULES AS EASTERN EMPEROR.
751 A.D.	THE MUSLIM ARMIES DEFEAT THE CHINESE ARMY AT THE BATTLE OF THE TALAS RIVER.
762 A.D.	THE ARAB EMPIRE MOVES ITS CAPITAL FROM DAMASCUS TO BAGHDAD AND LOOSES INTEREST IN WESTERN EUROPE.
775-780 A.D.	LEO IV RULES AS EASTERN EMPEROR.
780-797 A.D.	CONSTANTINE VI RULES AS EASTERN EMPEROR.
797-802 A.D.	IRENE RULES AS EASTERN EMPEROR.
800 A.D.	POPE LEO III SEPARATES FROM THE EASTERN EMPIRE AND DECLARES HIMSELF SUPREME BISHOP OF THE WEST.

802-811 A.D.	NICEPHORUS I RULES AS EASTERN EMPEROR.
802 A.D.	KHMER EMPIRE IS FOUNDED .
811 A.D.	STRAURACIUS RULES AS EASTERN EMPEROR.
811-813 A.D.	MICHEL I RULES AS EASTERN EMPEROR.
813-820 A.D.	LEO V RULES AS EASTERN EMPEROR.
820-829 A.D.	MICHAELII (PHRYGIAN DYNASTY) RULES AS EASTERN EMPEROR.
821-823 A.D.	THOMAS RULES AS EASTERN EMPEROR.
829 A.D.	THE FORTY-SIXTH YEAR OF JUBILEE.
829-839 A.D.	EGBERT, KING OF ESSEX, WINS ALLEGIANCE OF AND RULES ALL OF ENGLAND. HE IS A SAXON KING.
840 A.D.	DAN SETTLERS FOUND DUBLIN AND LIMERICK.
842-867 A.D.	MICHAEL III RULES AS EASTERN EMPEROR.
845 A.D.	A SEVERE PERSECUTION OF CHRISTIANS IN CHINA BREAKS OUT. THE SMALL CHRISTIAN COMMUNITY THERE IS SERIOUSLY WEAKENED.
851 A.D.	THE CANTERBURY CATHEDRAL IS SACKED BY THE DANES.
855 A.D.	ETHEL WULF OF WESSEX GOES WITH HIS SON ALFRED ON A PILGRIMAGE TO ROME .
858-860 A.D.	ETHEL BALD, SON OF ETHEL WULF, UNITES KENT AND WESSEX.
866-871 A.D.	ETHEL RED I, THIRD SON OF ETHEL WULF, BECOMES KING OF WESSEX AND FIGHTS THE DANES .
867-886 A.D.	BASIK I (MACEDONIAN DYNASTY) RULES AS EASTERN EMPEROR .
869-879 A.D.	CONSTANTINE RULES AS EASTERN EMPEROR.
871-899 A.D.	ALFRED THE GREAT, FOURTH SON OF ETHEL WULF, DEFEATS THE DANES AND FORTIFIES LONDON.

878 A.D.	CHRISTIAN PRESENCE STILL EXISTS IN PORT CITIES OF CHINA.
879 A.D.	THE FORTY-SEVENTH YEAR OF JUBILEE.
879 A.D.	THE POPE AND THE PATRIARCH OF CONSTANTINOPLE EXCOMMUNICATE EACH OTHER .
887-912 A.D.	LEO VI RULES AS EASTERN EMPEROR.
899-924 A.D.	EDWARD THE ELDER, SON OF ALFRED UNITES ENGLAND AND CLAIMS SCOTLAND.
912-913 A.D.	ALEXANDER RULES AS EASTERN EMPEROR.
913-959 A.D.	CONSTANTINE VII PORPHYGENITUS RULES AS EASTERN EMPEROR.
917 A.D.	BULGARIAN CHRISTIANS AS A GROUP OFFICIALLY SEPARATE FROM THE AUTHORITY OF ROMAN AND CONSTANTINOPLE.
904 A.D.	MAROZIA, MISTRESS TO POPE SERGIUS III, BECOMES THE MOTHER TO POPE JOHN XI (931-936). SHE IS ALSO AUNT OF POPE JOHN XIII (965-972) AND GRAND MOTHER OF POPE BENEDICT IV (973-974).
920-944 A.D.	ROMANUS I LECAPENUS RULES AS EASTERN EMPEROR.
921-931 A.D.	CHRISTOPHER RULES AS EASTERN EMPEROR.
924-940 A.D.	ATHELSTAN, THE GLORIOUS, EDWARD'S SON, RULES MERCIA AND WESSEX.
925-945 A.D.	STEPHEN RULES AS EASTERN EMPEROR.
929 A.D.	THE FORTY-EIGHTH YEAR OF JUBILEE.
940 A.D.	IKHSHIDIDS FIGHTS ABBASIDS AT LEJJUN NEAR MEGIDDO WITH NO VICTOR.
940-946 A.D.	EDMUND I, THIRD SON OF EDWARD, RULES MERCIA AND WESSEX.
946 A.D.	IKHSHIDIDS DEFEATS HAMDANIDS AT LEJJUN AND AKSAL NEAR MEGIDDO.

c950 A.D.	THE CANTERBURY CATHEDRAL IS REBUILT.
955-959 A.D.	EDWY THE FAIR, ELDEST SON OF EDMUND, RULES WESSEX.
959-963 A.D.	ROMANUS II RULES AS EASTERN EMPEROR.
959-975 A.D.	EDGAR THE PEACEFUL, SECOND SON OF EDMUND, RULES ALL ENGLAND.
963-969A.D.	NICEPHORUS II PHOCAS RULES AS EASTERN EMPEROR.
975 A.D.	THE BYZANTINES DEFEAT FATIMIDS AT MOUNT TABOR NEAR MEGGIDO.
976-1016 A.D.	ETHEL RED II, SECOND SON OF EDGAR RULES ENGLAND, MARRYING EMMA OF NORMANDY.
976-1025 A.D.	BASIL II RULES AS EASTERN EMPEROR.
979 A.D.	THE FORTY-NINTH YEAR OF JUBILEE.
987 A.D.	CATHOLIC MONKS REPORT THAT THEY CAN NOT FIND ANY CHRISTIANS IN CHINA.
c1000 A.D.	THE CHRISTIANS OF BRITAIN LAUNCH AN EVANGELISTIC EFFORT TO CONVERT THE VIKINGS.THEY ALSO OUTLAW THE PRESENCE OF CATHOLIC PRIESTS IN BRITAIN. CHRISTIANS WHO DISAGREED RELIGIOUSLY WITH ROMAN (PAPAL) AUTHORITY OVER THE CHURCH WERE NUMEROUS IN ITALY, SPAIN, GAUL, AND GERMANY, AND SUFFERED OCCASIONAL LOCAL PERSECUTIONS.
1016 A.D.	EDMUND II, SON OF ETHEL RED II, RULES LONDON.
1016-1035 A.D.	CANUTE THE DANE MARRIES EMMA, GIVES WESSEX TO EDMUND.
1022 A.D.	DISAGREEMENT WITH CATHOLIC RELIGIOUS RULE OFTEN TREATED AS A CAPITAL OFFENSE.
1025-1028 A.D.	CONSTANTINE VIII (IX) RULES AS EASTERN EMPEROR.

1028-1034 A.D.	ROMANUS III ARGYRUS RULES AS EASTERN EMPEROR.
1029 A.D.	THE FIFTIETH YEAR OF JUBILEE.
1034-1041 A.D.	MICHAEL IV, THE PAPHLAGONIAN, RULES AS EASTERN EMPEROR.
1035-1040 A.D.	HAROLD I, OF CANUTE, RULES ENGLAND.
1041-1042 A.D.	MICHAEL V CALAPHATES RULES AS EASTERN EMPEROR.
1042-1066 A.D.	EDWARD, SON OF ETHEL RED II, RULES ENGLAND.
1042 A.D.	ZOE AND THOEDORA RULE IN THE EAST.
1042-1055 A.D.	CONSTANTINE IX MONOMCHUS RULES IN THE EAST
c1050 A.D.	MOSLEM SELJUK TURKS COME FROM CENTRAL ASIA, PASS THROUGH PERSIA, AND STRENGTHEN BAGHDAD.
1055-1056 A.D.	THEODORA RULES THE EASTERN EMPIRE.
1056-1057 A.D.	MICHAEL VI STRATIOTICUS RULES AS EASTERN EMPEROR.
1057-1059 A.D.	ISAAC I COMNENOS RULES AS EASTERN EMPEROR.
1059-1067 A.D.	CONSTANTINE X (IX) DUCAS RULES AS EASTERN EMPEROR.
c1062 A.D.	MOSLEM SELJUK TURKS FROM PERSIA AND BAGHDAD CROSS THE EUPHRATES RIVER AND THEN INVADE ASIA MINOR AND ARMENIA.
1066 A.D.	HAROLD II, EDWARD'S BROTHER-IN-LAW TAKES THE THROWN OF ENGLAND, BUT WILLIAM OF NORMANDY, A FRENCH CATHOLIC, CONQUERS ENGLAND.
1066-1087 A.D.	WILLIAM I OF NORMANDY RULES ENGLAND.
1066-1534 A.D.	THE BRITISH ISLES, WITH MUCH RESISTANCE, ENDURES CATHOLIC RULE.
1068-1071 A.D.	ROMANUS IV DIOGENES RULES AS EASTERN EMPEROR.

1071 A.D.	THE BYZANTINE ARMY IS CRUSHED AT MANZIKERT.
1071-1078 A.D.	MICHAEL VII DUCAS RULES AS EASTERN EMPEROR.
1078-1081 A.D.	NICEPHORUS III BONTANIATES, NICEPHORUS BYRENNIUS, AND NICEPHORUS BASILACIUS RULE AS EASTERN EMPERORS.
1079 A.D.	FIFTY-FIRST YEAR OF JUBILEE.
1080-1081 A.D.	NICEPHORUS MELISSENUS RULES AS EASTERN EMPEROR.
1081-1118 A.D.	ALEXIUS I COMNENUS (COMMNENI DYNASTY) RULES AS EASTERN EMPEROR.
1087-1100 A.D.	WILLIAM II, THIRD SON OF WILLIAM I, RULES ENGLAND.
1099 A.D.	THE FIRST OF MANY CATHOLIC CRUSADES LAUNCHED TO TURN BACK THE TURKISH MOSLEMS.
1100-1135 A.D.	HENRY I, YOUNGEST SON OF WILLIAM I, RULES ENGLAND.
1113 A.D.	MAUDUD DEFEATS THE CRUSADERS AT MOUNT TABOR NEAR MEGGIDO.
1118-1143 A.D.	JOHN II COMENUS RULES AS EASTERN EMPEROR.
1129 A.D.	FIFTY-SECOND YEAR OF JUBILEE.
1135-1154 A.D.	STEPHEN OF BLOIS, SON OF A DAUGHTER OF WILLIAM I RULES ENGLAND.
1143-1180 A.D.	MANUEL I RULES AS EASTERN EMPEROR.
1150-1200 A.D.	CATHOLIC WRITERS CLAIM NON-CATHOLIC CHRISTIANITY "NOT ONLY MENACED THE CHURCH'S (CATHOLIC) EXISTENCE, BUT UNDERMINED THE VERY FOUNDATION OF CHRISTIAN (CATHOLIC) SOCIETY" THROUGHOUT GERMANY, FRANCE, AND SPAIN. NUMEROUS NON-CATHOLIC CHRISTIANS WERE BURNED AT THE STAKE.

1154-1189 A.D.	HENRY II, SON OF A DAUGHTER OF HENRY I, RULES ENGLAND.
1179 A.D.	FIFTY-THIRD YEAR OF JUBILEE
1180-1183 A.D.	ALEIUS II RULES AS EASTERN EMPEROR.
1182 A.D.	SALADIN DEFEATS THE DABURIYANS AT DABURIYA AND THEN DEFEATS THE CRUSADERS AT FORBELET NEAR MEGIDDO.
1183-1185 A.D.	ANDRONICUS I RULES AS EASTERN EMPEROR.
1183-1191 A.D.	ISAAC RULES AS EMPEROR OF CYPRUS.
1183 A.D.	SALADIN AND THE CRUSADERS FIGHT AT AYN JALUT NEAR MEGIDDO, BUT THERE IS NO CLEAR VICTOR.
1185-1195 A.D.	ISAAC II (ANGELI DYNASTY) RULES AS EASTERN EMPEROR.
1187 A.D.	SALADIN DEFEATS THE CRUSADERS AT MOUNT TABOR, DABURIYA, ZARIN AND AL-FULA NEAR MEGGIDO.
1189-1199 A.D.	RICHARD THE LION HEARTED, A CRUSADER, SON OF HENRY II, RULES ENGLAND. THIS IS THE TIME OF ROBINHOOD.
1195-1203 A.D.	ALEXIUS III RULES AS EASTERN EMPEROR.
1199-1216 A.D.	JOHN, SON OF HENRY II, RULES ENGLAND.
1203-1204 A.D.	ISAAC II (RESTORED) WITH ALEXIUS IV RULES AS EASTERN EMPEROR.
1204 A.D.	ALEXIUS V DUCAS MURTZUPHLUS RULES AS EASTERN EMPEROR.
1204-1222 A.D.	THEODORE I LASCARIS (LASCARID DUNASTY) RULES AS EASTERN EMPEROR.
1206-1227 A.D.	MONGOLIANS UNDER GENGHIS KHAN CONQUER CHINA, AFGHANISTAN, AND MUCH OF IRAN (PERSIA). THE DESCENDANTS OF MAGOG STRETCH THEIR EMPIRE FROM SHANGHAI TO BUDAPEST. THE CAPITOL CITY WAS

	KHANBALIK (LATER KNOWN AS PEKING AND THEN BEIJING).
1209 A.D.	THE POPE ORDERS A CRUSADE AGAINST CHRISTIANS IN SOUTHERN FRANCE WHO DENY HIS AUTHORITY.
1215 A.D.	FOURTH LATERN COUNCIL PROVIDES SPECIAL LAWS AND PUNISHMENT FOR CHRISTIANS WHO DISAGREE WITH CATHOLIC LEADERSHIP.
1215 A.D.	ENGLISHMEN REVOLT AND FORCE JOHN TO SIGN THE MAGNA CARTA. THIS GRANTED FREE MEN DUE PROCESS OF LAW. NOBLES WERE GIVEN RIGHTS THAT THE KING COULD NOT TAKE AWAY.
1216-1272 A.D.	HENRY III, SON OF JOHN, BEGINS TO RULES ENGLAND AT NINE YEARS OF AGE.
1217 A.D.	THE MOSLEMS DEFEAT THE CRUSADERS AT MOUNT TABOR NEAR MEGIDDO.
1222-1254 A.D.	JOHN III DUCAS VATATZES RULES AS EASTERN EMPEROR.
1229 A.D.	FIFTY-FOURTH YEAR OF JUBILEE.
1252 A.D.	INNOCENT IV AUTHORIZES TORTURE OF CHRISTIANS TO GET CONFESSIONS AND INFORMATION ABOUT THOSE WHO DO NOT FOLLOW CATHOLIC VIEWS.
1254-1258 A.D.	THEODORE II LASCARIS RULES AS EASTERN EMPEROR.
1258-1261 A.D.	JOHN IV LASCARIS RULES AS EASTERN EMPEROR.
1259-1282 A.D.	MICHAEL VIII PALEOLOGUS (PALEOLOGI DYNASTY) RULES AS EASTERN EMPEROR.
1260 A.D.	MAMLUKES DEFEATS THE MONGOLS AT 'AYN JALUT NEAR MEGIDDO.
1263 A.D.	MAMLUKES DEFEATS THE HOSPITALLERS AT MOUNT TABOR NEAR MEGIDDO.
1264 A.D.	THE HOSPITALLERS AND TEMPLARS DEFEAT MAMLUKES AT LEJJUN NEAR MEGIDDO.

1272-1307 A.D.	EDWARD I, SON OF HENRY III, RULES ENGLAND.
1279 A.D.	THE FIFTY FITH YEAR OF JUBILEE.
1279 A.D.	KHUBILAI KHAN ESTABLISHES HIS MONGOLIAN ADMINISTRATION AND BECOMES EMPEROR OF ALL OF CHINA. MONGOLIANS (THE SONS OF MAGOG) BECOME THE RULING CLASS OF CHINA.
1281 A.D.	KHUBILAI KHAN TRIES TO CONQUER JAPAN WITH 150,000 SOLDIERS. A STORM CALLED "KAMIKAZE" DESTROYS HIS FLEET AND SAVES JAPAN.
1282-1328 A.D	ANDRONICUS II RULES AS EASTERN EMPEROR.
1300 A.D.	TURKISH MUSLIMS, WHO HAD SETTLED IN ASIA MINOR, BEGIN FORMING THE OTTOMAN EMPIRE.
1307-1327 A.D.	EDWARD II, SON OF EDWARD I, RULES ENGLAND, BUT IS EVENTUALLY DEPOSED BY PARLIAMENT.
1327-1377 A.D.	EDWARD III, SON OF EDWARD II, RULES ENGLAND.
1328-1341 A.D.	ANDRONICUS III RULES AS EASTERN EMPEROR.
1329 A.D.	THE FIFTY-SIXTH YEAR OF JUBILEE.
1341-1391 A.D.	JOHN V (RESTORED) RULES AS EASTERN EMEROR.
1347-1352 A.D.	THE BLACK DEATH (BUBONIC PLAGUE) KILLS 1/3 OF EUROPE. (OVER 23,000,000 PEOPLE)
1351 A.D.	ENGLAND PASSES A LAW THAT FORBIDS THE POPE TO INTERFERE IN THE CHOOSING OF CHURCH OFFICIALS.
1353 A.D.	ENGLAND PASSED A LAW PROHIBITING LEGAL APPEALS TO THE POPE OR ANY OTHER COURT OUTSIDE ENGLAND.
1377-1400 A.D.	RICHARD II, GRANDSON OF EDWARD III, RULES ENGLAND UNTIL HE IS DEPOSED.

1378-1417 A.D.	CATHOLIC CHURCH IS DIVIDED BETWEEN TWO POPES. ONE RESIDES IN ROME, THE OTHER IN AVIGNON , FRANCE.
1379 A.D.	THE FIFTY-SEVENTH YEAR OF JUBILEE.
1390 A.D.	JOHN VII RULES AS EASTERN EMPEROR.
1391-1425 A.D.	MANUEL II RULES AS EASTERN EMPEROR.
1399-1413 A.D.	HENRY IV, OF THE HOUSE OF LANCASTER, RULES ENGLAND.
1413-1422 A.D.	HENRY V, SON OF HENRY IV, RULES ENGLAND.
1422-1471 A.D.	HENRY VI, SON OF HENRY V, RULES ENGLAND UNTIL DEPOSED IN 1461. HE DIES IMPRISONED IN THE TOWER OF LONDON.
1425-1448 A.D.	JOHN VIII RULES AS EASTERN EMPEROR.
1429 A.D.	THE FIFTY-EIGHTH YEAR OF JUBILEE.
1434-1499 A.D.	PORTUGAL EXPLORES AFRICA AND INDIA.
1438 A.D.	TYPE CASTING IS INVENTED IN GERMANY. THE FIRST PRINTING PRESS BEGINS OPERATION.
1449-1453 A.D.	CONSTANTINE XI (XIII) DRAGASES RULES AS EASTERN EMPEROR.
1453 A.D.	CONSTANTINOPLE FALLS TO OTTOMAN CANNONS.

CHAPTER NINE
A CHRISTIAN CHRONOLOGY OF HISTORY
(1453 A.D. – 1858 A.D.)
A TIME LINE OF HUMAN HISTORY
FROM A CHRISTIAN PROSPECTIVE
Compiled by "God's Friend"

1455 A.D.	FIRST BIBLE PRINTED ON A PRINTING PRESS.
1461-1483 A.D.	EDWARD IV, GREAT-GRANDSON OF EDWARD III, RULES ENGLAND.
1479 A.D.	THE FIFTY-NINTH YEAR OF JUBILEE.
1485-1509 A.D.	HENRY VII UNITES LANCASTER AND YORK BY MARRIAGE, AND RULES ENGLAND.
1492 A.D.	COLUMBUS DISCOVERS AMERICA. ALL JEWS ARE EXPELLED FROM SPAIN UNDER PENALTY OF DEATH, NEVER TO RETURN.
1492-1522 A.D.	SPAIN EXPLORES CENTRAL AND SOUTH AMERICA AND SAILS AROUND THE WORLD.
1494 A.D.	POPE ALEXANDER I DIVIDES THE WORLD BETWEEN SPAIN AND PORTUGAL AND THE TWO COUNTRIES SIGN THE TREATY OF TORDESILLAS. THOMAS TORQUEMADA IS MADE INQUISITOR-GENERAL OF ALL SPAIN.
1495 A.D.	ALL JEWS ARE EXPELLED FROM PORTUGAL. LEONARDO DAVINCI BEGINS PAINTING "THE LAST SUPPER."
1506 A.D.	POPE JULIUS II STARTS BUILDING ST. PETER'S CATHEDRAL AND AUTHORIZES

	THE SALE OF INDULGENCES TO FINANCE IT.
1508-1509 A.D.	MICHELANGELO BEGINS PAINTING THE CEILING OF THE SISTINE CHAPEL. THE FIRST NEGRO SLAVES ARE BROUGHT TO AMERICA.
1509-1547 A.D.	HENRY VIII, SON OF HENRY VII, RULES ENGLAND.
1512 A.D.	CATHOLICS ADOPT THE NAME, "CHURCH OF MALIGNANTS," FOR CHRISTIANS OUTSIDE THE CATHOLIC CHURCH. COPERNICUS CHALLENGES CATHOLIC DOCTRINE, SAYING THE EARTH AND OTHER PLANETS REVOLVE AROUND THE SUN.
1514 A.D.	CARDINAL XIMENES PUBLISHES THE FIRST POLYGLOT BIBLE IN HEBREW, CHALDEE, GREEK, AND LATIN.
1516 A.D.	ERASMUS PUBLISHES HIS GREEK NEW TESTAMENT.
1517 A.D.	MARTIN LUTHER PUBLISHES 95 OBJECTIONS TO CATHOLIC PRACTICES AND PROTESTS THE SALE OF INDULGENCES. EGYPT IS CONQUERED BY THE OTTOMAN TURKS.
1519 A.D.	ZWINGLI IS CONVERTED WHILE PASTOR AT ZURICH, AND BEGINS THE SWISS REFORMATION. HORSES ARE BROUGHT TO NORTH AMERICA BY CORTEZ.
1521 A.D.	THE AZTECS SURRENDER TO THE SPANISH. AT THE DIET OF WORMS CHARLES V ANNOUNCES WAR AGAINST LUTHER AND CHRISTIANS DEFYING THE POPES AUTHORITY.
1524 A.D.	FRANCE BEGINS TO EXPLORE AMERICA (CANADA).
1526 A.D.	TYNDALE'S TRANSLATION OF THE BIBLE IS PUBLISHED. CHARLES V. EMPEROR OF SPAIN, AMERICA, SICILY, NAPLES, AND

	THE NETHERLANDS, SACKS ROME AND TAKES THE POPE PRISONER.
1529 A.D.	THE SIXTIETH YEAR OF JUBILEE.
1530 A.D.	LUTHER'S TRANSLATION OF THE BIBLE IS PUBLISHED.
1534 A.D.	HENRY VIII BREAKS FROM THE CATHOLIC CHURCH AND ESTABLISHES HIMSELF AS HEAD OF THE CHURCH OF ENGLAND. HE KEEPS MUCH OF THE STRUCTURE OF THE CATHOLIC CHURCH. THE ARCHBISHOP OF CANTERBURY BECOMES ADMINISTRATIVE HEAD OF THE CHURCH OF ENGLAND.
1536 A.D.	JOHN CALVIN BEGINS A REFORM MOVEMENT IN GENEVA. THE AUTHORITY OF THE POPE IS DECLARED VOID IN ENGLAND.
1546-1555 A.D.	WAR BETWEEN THE CATHOLIC AND LUTHERAN PRINCES OF GERMANY ENDS WITH THE PEACE OF AUGSBURG THAT PERMITTED EACH PRINCE TO CHOOSE THE RELIGION ALLOWED IN HIS DOMAIN. THIS GAVE NO RELIEF TO MANY CHRISTIANS.
1547-1553 A.D.	EDWARD VI, SON OF HENRY VIII, RULES ENGLAND. HE RULED UNDER REGENTS. HE NAMED LADY JANE GREY HIS SUCCESSOR, BUT SHE RULED ONLY 9 DAYS BEING REPLACED BY MARY I WHO HAD HER BEHEADED.
1553-1558 A.D.	BLOODY MARY BECOMES QUEEN OF ENGLAND, MARRIES PHILIP II, KING OF SPAIN, AND TRIES TO FORCE ENGLAND TO BE CATHOLIC.
1558-1603 A.D.	ELIZABETH I BECOMES A RALLYING POINT FOR PROTESTANTS, AND THEN QUEEN OF ENGLAND. SHE REESTABLISHED THE CHURCH OF

	ENGLAND, AND SOME TOLERANCE FOR NON-CATHOLIC GROUPS. MARY IS EXECUTED IN 1587.
1572 A.D.	THE INCAS SURRENDER TO THE SPANISH. CATHOLICS IN FRANCE KILL OVER 20,000 NON-CATHOLIC CHRISTIANS FOR FEAR THEY WILL COME TO POWER.
1558 A.D.	DEFEAT OF SPANISH ARMADA BREAKS THE BACK OF CATHOLIC NAVAL POWER.
1598 A.D.	HENRY IV OF FRANCE GRANTS NON-CATHOLIC CHRISTIANS THE SAME RIGHTS AS CATHOLIC CHRISTIANS (THE EDICT OF NANTES). HENRY IV WAS ONE OF THE CHRISTIANS PERSECUTED IN 1572. HE RECEIVED HIS THROWN ONLY AFTER PROMISING TO BE A CATHOLIC.
1603-1625 A.D.	JAMES I, SON OF BLOODY MARY, ALLY OF ELIZABETH I, BECOMES NON-CATHOLIC KING OF ENGLAND.
1607 A.D.	ENGLAND ESTABLISHES HER FIRST AMERICAN COLONY.
1608 A.D.	FRANCE SETTLES QUEBEC, FORBIDDING NON-CATHOLICS THE RIGHT TO GO THERE.
1610 A.D.	HENRY IV OF FRANCE IS ASSASSINATED FOR HIS PART IN THE EDICT OF NANTES.
1615 A.D.	KING JAMES AUTHORIZES AN ENGLISH TRANSLATION OF THE BIBLE.
1620 A.D.	NON-CATHOLIC, NON-CHURCH OF ENGLAND, CHRISTIANS, WANTING RELIGIOUS FREEDOM, SETTLE AMERICA, ARRIVING IN NEW ENGLAND ABOARD THE MAYFLOWER. ONE OF THOSE PILGRAMS WAS MARY SINGLETON. THEY WERE FOLLOWED BY NUMEROUS OTHERS OF SIMILAR RELIGIOUS BELIEFS. ONLY TWO BRITISH COLONIES, GEORGIA (A PENAL COLONY) AND

	MARYLAND (A CATHOLIC COLONY), ARE EXCEPTIONS.
1624 A.D.	THE DUTCH ESTABLISH COLONIES IN NORTH AMERICA CALLED "NEW NETHERLANDS."
1625-1649 A.D.	CHARLES I, KING OF ENGLAND, SCOTLAND, AND IRELAND, BEGAN HIS RULE BY OFFENDING THE ENGLISH PUBLIC BY MARRYING A CATHOLIC. HE WAS LATER CONVICTED OF TREASON AND BEHEADED BY LEADERS OF THE ENGLISH PARLIAMENT.
1628 A.D.	CHARLES I FORCED TO AGREE TO PETITION OF RIGHTS. TAXES COULD NOT BE RAISED WITHOUT PARLIAMENT'S APPROVAL.
1629 A.D.	THE SIXTY-FOURTH YEAR OF JUBILEE.
1629-1640 A.D.	CHARLES I GOVERNS WITHOUT CALLING PARLIAMENT INTO SESSION.
1640 A.D.	ATTEMPTING TO FORCE THE SCOTS TO BE MEMBERS OF THE CHURCH OF ENGLAND, CHARLES NEEDS WAR FUNDS AND CALLS PARLIAMENT INTO SESSION TO RAISE TAXES. NON-CATHOLIC, NON-CHURCH OF ENGLAND CHRISTIANS DOMINATE PARLIAMENT AND PASS LAWS PROTECTING THEMSELVES, INCLUDING FREEDOM FROM RELIGIOUS OR POLITICAL PERSECUTION. THIS LAYS THE GROUND WORK FOR RELIGIOUS FREEDOM THROUGHOUT THE BRITISH EMPIRE. THE EMPIRE WAS TO SPAN THE GLOBE AND INCLUDE SUCH DISTANT PLACES AS GREAT BRITAIN, IRELAND, SCOTLAND, NORMANDY IN FRANCE, THE AMERICAN COLONIES, THE BRITISH INDIES, NEWFOUNDLAND, AUSTRALIA, CANADA, SOUTH AFRICA, KENYA,

UGANDA, TANGANYIKA, ZANZIBAR, CEYLON, MALTA, CAPE OF GOOD HOPE, NEW ZEALAND, BURMA, MALAYA, NEW GUINEA, PAKISTAN, CYPRUS, GIBRALTAR, BRITISH SOMALI LAND, RHODESIA, SARAWAK, SINGAPORE, FIJI, THE BRITISH SOLOMON ISLANDS, BORNEO, INDIA, EGYPT, HONG KONG, AND MANY MORE. ENGLAND'S EMPIRE GREW TO CONTROL A FOURTH OF THE WORLD. THEIR POLICIES INFLUENCE MUCH OF THE REST OF THE WORLD. THIS IS THE BEGINNING OF THE ELIMINATION OF FORCED STATE RELIGION. IT ENDS 1260 YEARS OF CORRUPT, "CHRISTIAN" STATE CHURCHES.

1642-1649 A.D.   KING CHARLES IGNORED SOME OF THE PASSED LAWS. NON-CATHOLIC, NON-CHURCH OF ENGLAND CHRISTIANS FOUGHT FOR THEIR RIGHTS OF SELF-GOVERNMENT AND RELIGIOUS FREEDOM, WINNING AND BEHEADING CHARLES, HEAD OF THE CHURCH OF ENGLAND. CHARLES WAS ALSO UNPOPULAR BECAUSE HE WANTED TO INTERMARRY HIS LINEAGE WITH CATHOLIC EUROPEAN ROYALTY. OLIVER CROMWELL LEADS THE LIBERATING ARMY.

1652-1658 A.D.   OLIVER CROMWELL RULES ENGLAND AS LORD PROTECTOR.

1658-1659 A.D.   RICHARD CROMWELL, SON OF OLIVER, RULES ENGLAND. HE RESIGNED ON MAY 5, 1659.

1660-1685 A.D.   CHARLES II, SON OF CHARLES I, RULES ENGLAND.

1662-1690 A.D.   ENGLAND ESTABLISHES TRADE COLONIES IN INDIA.

1664 A.D.	THE DUTCH LOOSE NEW NETHERLANDS TO ENGLAND.
1673-1683 A.D.	POLAND SMASHES THE OTTOMAN TURKS AT THE BATTLE OF CHOCZIM AND VIENNA.
1674 A.D.	FRANCE ESTABLISHES A TRADE COLONY IN INDIA.
1679 A.D.	THE SIXTY-THIRD YEAR OF JUBILEE.
1685 A.D.	LOUIS XIV OF FRANCE ABOLISHES THE EDICT OF NANTES.
1685-1689 A.D.	JAMES II, SON OF CHARLES I, RULES ENGLAND, BUT IS DEPOSED.
1689 A.D.	UNWILLING TO ENDURE A CATHOLIC KING (THE HEIR APPARENT), PARLIAMENT ASKED WILLIAM OF ORANGE (A NON-CATHOLIC CHRISTIAN), KING OF THE NETHERLANDS TO COME RULE ENGLAND. THE AGREEMENT WORKED OUT RESULTED IN THE ESTABLISHMENT OF A CONSTITUTIONAL MONARCHY AND CONTINUED RELIGIOUS FREEDOM.
1689-1702 A.D.	WILLIAM III (WILLIAM OF ORANGE) AND HIS WIFE, MARY II, DAUGHTER OF JAMES II, RULE ENGLAND.
1689-1763 A.D.	THE FRENCH AND INDIAN WARS IN AMERICA RESULT IN ENGLAND GAINING CONTROL OF CANADA AND LAND WEST OF THE THIRTEEN AMERICAN COLONIES.
1692 A.D.	THE CHURCH OF ENGLAND BECOMES THE ESTABLISHED CHURCH OF MARYLAND AND THE SALARIES OF THEIR CLERGY ARE PAID BY TAXES UNTIL THE END OF THE REVOLUTIONARY WAR.
1702-1714 A.D.	ANNE, SECOND DAUGHTER OF JAMES II, RULES ENGLAND.

1714-1727 A.D.	GEORGE I OF THE HOUSE OF HANOVER RULES ENGLAND.
1729 A.D.	SIXTY-FOURTH YEAR OF JUBILEE.
1735 A.D.	ZAHIR AL-UMAR DEFEATS THE NABLUS-SAQR ALLIANCE AT AL-RAWDAH NEAR MEGIDDO.
1767-1820 A.D.	GEORGE II, SON OF GEORGE I, RULES ENGLAND.
1763 A.D.	THE ENGLISH DRIVE THE FRENCH FROM INDIA AND CANADA.
1765 A.D.	THE ENGLISH KING IMPOSES THE STAMP ACT ON THE AMERICAN COLONIES.
1771-1773 A.D.	ZAHIR AL-UMAR DEFEATS LEJJUN AT LEJJUN NEAR MEGIDDO.
1773 A.D.	THE BOSTON TEA PARTY IS LED BY SAMUEL ADAMS, A COUSIN OF JOHN ADAMS.
1775-1783 A.D.	THE AMERICAN REVOLUTIONARY WAR TAKES PLACE. THIS TURNS THE THIRTEEN AMERICAN COLONIES INTO THE UNITED STATES OF AMERICAN.
1776 A.D.	THE UNITED STATES DECLARATION OF INDEPENDENCE RECOGNIZES THAT GOD RULES ABOVE GOVERNMENTS AND RECOGNIZES INDIVIDUAL'S GOD GIVEN RIGHTS THAT GOVERNMENTS HAVE NO RIGHT TO INTERFERE WITH. IT IS WRITTEN BY A COMMITTEE THAT INCLUDED THOMAS JEFFERSON AND JOHN ADAMS. JOHN ADAMS IS THE SEVEN TIMES GREAT GRANDFATHER OF BILL SINGLETON. HE WAS ALSO THE FATHER OF JOHN QUINCY ADAMS.
1779 A.D.	THE SIXTY-FITH YEAR OF JUBILEE.
1781 A.D.	RICHARD STOCKTON, THE FATHER OF RICHARD STOCKTON (STOCKTON, CA. WAS NAMED AFTER HIM), DIRECTED HIS CHILDREN IN HIS LAST WILL AND

	TESTAMENT, "WITH THE LAST WORD OF THEIR FATHER, I THINK PROPER HERE, NOT ONLY TO SUBSCRIBE TO THE ENTIRE BELIEF OF THE GREAT LEADING DOCTRINE OF THE CHRISTIAN RELIGION... BUT ALSO IN THE HEART OF A FATHER'S AFFECTION, TO CHARGE AND EXHORT THEM TO REMEMBER THAT THE FEAR OF THE LORD IS THE BEGINNING OF WISDOM."
1784 A.D.	JOHN WESLEY ARRIVES IN NEW YORK AND STARTS THE METHODIST EPISCOPAL CHURCH IN AMERICA. THE ORGANIZATION IS NOT ACCORDING TO BIBLE TEACHING. WESLEY TEACHES THAT THE BIBLE SHOULD BE THE ONLY AUTHORITY. HE CALLS PEOPLE TO BECOME "DOWN RIGHT BIBLE CHRISTIANS."
1786 A.D.	ALEXANDER CAMBELL IS BORN IN NORTHERN IRELAND. HIS COMMUNITY IS PREDOMINANTLY ANGLO-SCOTTISH PROTESTANT. HIS FATHER IS A PRESBYTERIAN SCHOOL TEACHER AND HE LATER FOLLOWS IN HIS FATHER'S OCCUPATION.
1787 A.D.	THE UNITED STATES CONSTITUTION IS ESTABLISHED AS THE HIGHEST HUMAN LAW FOR THE UNITED STATES. IT RECOGNIZES THAT HUMAN GOVERNMENTS ARE BELOW GOD IN AUTHORITY. IT ALSO RECOGNIZES THE INDIVIDUAL'S FREEDOM OF RELIGION. JOHN ADAMS HELPS AUTHOR IT.
1788 A.D.	ENGLAND ESTABLISHES AUSTRALIA AS A PENAL COLONY. GEORGE WASHINGTON, THE FIRST PRESIDENT OF THE UNITED STATES, ISSUES A NATIONAL DAY OF THANKSGIVING PROCLAMATION

	STATING, "IT IS THE DUTY OF ALL NATIONS TO ACKNOWLEDGE THE PROVIDENCE OF ALMIGHTY GOD, TO OBEY HIS WILL, TO BE GRATEFUL FOR HIS BENEFITS, AND HUMBLY IMPLORE HIS PROTECTION AND FAVOR...." GEORGE WASHINGTON CHOOSES JOHN ADAMS AS HIS VICE-PRESIDENT.
1789-1799 A.D.	THE FRENCH REVOLUTION AND REIGN OF TERROR BEGINS IN WHICH FRANCE LOOSES MANY OF HER BEST MINDS, BUT GAINS SOME FREEDOM FOR THE COMMON MAN.
1793 A.D.	FREE ENGLISH SETTLERS BEGIN TO ARRIVE IN AUSTRALIA.
1795 A.D.	JAMES HUTTON LAYS THE EARLY BASIS FOR "UNIFORMITARIANISM" IN EVOLUTIONARY GEOLOGY. HE SAYS THAT IN GEOLOGY ALL THINGS HAVE ALWAYS PROCEEDED THE SAME. OUR PLANET IS THE RESULT OF GRADUALLY DEVELOPING PROCESSES UNINFLUENCED BY A GREAT CATASTROPHE (SEE 63-68 A.D.). THIS MISUNDERSTANDING OF OUR PLANET'S HISTORY FULFILLS THE PROPHESY OF 2 PETER 3:3-10 AND OFFERS THE BASIS FOR BAD SCIENCE THAT CAN MISINTERPRET GEOLOGY TO SUPPORT EVOLUTIONARY THEORY.
1799-1815 A.D.	THE NAPOLEONIC WARS RAGE IN EUROPE.
1799 A.D.	NAPOLEON DEFEATS THE OTTOMANS AT MOUNT TABOR NEAR MEGIDDO.
1804 A.D.	THE PRESBYTERIAN SYNODS BEGIN MARKING SOME PREACHERS AS HERETICS RESULTING IN A GROUP OF PREACHERS, INCLUDING BARTON W. STONE, FORMING AN INDEPENDENT

SYNOD. THEY DECLARE THEIR TOTAL ABANDONMENT OF ALL AUTHORITATIVE CREEDS, EXCEPT THE BIBLE. IN LESS THAN A YEAR 15 CONGREGATIONS ARE ESTABLISHED. THE INDEPENDENT (SPRINGFIELD) SYNOD DECIDES ITS OWN EXISTENCE IS AN ADDITION TO BIBLE ORGANIZATION AND DISSOLVES ITSELF. THIS GROUP EXPRESSES A SINCERE AND HONEST DESIRE TO GIVE UP EVERYTHING OF HUMAN ORIGIN IN RELIGION AND TAKE ONLY THE BIBLE. THIS BECOMES THE MARK OF THE AMERICAN RESTORATION MOVEMENT. THOMAS JEFFERSON, THE THIRD PRESIDENT OF THE UNITED STATES, WRITES, "I CONSIDER THE DOCTRINES OF JESUS, AS DELIVERED BY HIM, TO CONTAIN THE OUTLINES OF THE SUBLIMEST SYSTEM OF MORALITY THAT HAS EVER BEEN TAUGHT....."

1807 A.D. THOMAS CAMBELL, FATHER OF ALEXANDER, COMES TO AMERICA AND BEGINS CIRCUIT PREACHING FOR THE CHARTERS PRESBYTERY.

1808 A.D. THOMAS CAMBELL IS DISMISSED BY THE PRESBYTERIAN SYNOD BECAUSE OF CHARGES THAT HE TAUGHT THERE WAS NOTHING BUT HUMAN AUTHORITY FOR CREEDS AND CONFESSIONS OF FAITH. HE FEELS THAT THE HOLY SCRIPTURES, DIVINELY INSPIRED, ARE ALL SUFFICIENT.
HE BEGINS PREACHING TO GATHERINGS AND COINS THE MOTTO: "WHERE THE BIBLE SPEAKS, WE SPEAK, WHERE THE BIBLE IS SILENT, WE ARE SILENT."

1809A.D. ALEXANDER CAMBELL JOINS HIS FATHER IN AMERICA AFTER GRADUATING

FROM GLASGOW UNIVERSITY. JAMES
MADISON, THE FOURTH PRESIDENT OF
THE UNITED STATES AND A LEADER IN
WRITING THE CONSTITUTION, SAYS, "WE
HAVE ALL BEEN ENCOURAGED TO FEEL
THE GUARDIANSHIP AND GUIDANCE
OF THAT ALMIGHTY BEING, WHOSE
POWER REGULATES THE DESTINY OF
NATIONS...."

1811 A.D.   JOHN QUINCY ADAMS, SIXTH
PRESIDENT OF THE UNITED STATES
WRITES, "SO GREAT IS MY VENERATION
FOR THE BIBLE, AND SO STRONG
MY BELIEF, THAT WHEN DULY READ
AND MEDITATED ON, IT IS OF ALL
BOOKS IN THE WORLD, THAT WHICH
CONTRIBUTES MOST TO MAKE MEN
GOOD, WISE, AND HAPPY......."

1813 A.D.   ALEXANDER CAMBELL PREACHES FOR
THE BRUSH RUN CHURCH WHICH JOINS
THE REDSTONE ASSOCIATION OF BAPTIST
CHURCHES UPON THE CONDITION
THAT IT CAN TEACH WHAT IT BELIEVES
THE BIBLE TEACHES. JOHN ADAMS, THE
SECOND PRESIDENT OF THE UNITED
STATES, WRITES, "I HAVE EXAMINED ALL
RELIGIONS, AS WELL AS MY NARROW
SPHERE, MY STRAIGHTENED MEANS, AND
MY BUSY LIFE WOULD ALLOW, AND THE
RESULT IS THAT THE BIBLE IS THE BEST
BOOK IN THE WORLD..."

1818 A.D.   WALTER SCOTT, AFTER GRADUATION
FROM EDINBURGH UNIVERSITY, LANDS
IN NEW YORK AND BECOMES A LATIN
TEACHER.

1820-1830 A.D.   GEORGE IV, ELDEST SON OF GEORGE III,
RULES ENGLAND.

1820 A.D.   ALEXANDER CAMBELL HOLDS HIS FIRST
DEBATE. IT IS ON THE SUBJECT AND

MODE OF BAPTISM. HIS OPPONENT
IS JOHN WALKER, A PRESBYTERIAN
PREACHER. THIS IS THE FIRST OF MANY
DEBATES ON VARIOUS SUBJECTS THAT
HAVE AN IMPACT ON THE BELIEF OF
MILLIONS.

1821 A.D.   BARTON W. STONE COMES TO REALIZE
THAT THE BIBLE TEACHES BAPTISM BY
IMMERSION OF PENITENT BELIEVERS
FOR THE REMISSION OF SINS. JOHN
QUINCY ADAMS, THE SIXTH PRESIDENT
OF THE UNITED STATES, DECLARES,
"THE HIGHEST GLORY OF THE
AMERICAN REVOLUTION WAS THIS; IT
CONNECTED IN ONE INDISSOLUBLE
BOND THE PRINCIPLES OF CIVIL
GOVERNMENT WITH THE PRINCIPLES
OF CHRISTIANITY."

1823 A.D.   ALEXANDER CAMPBELL BEGINS
PUBLISHING THE "CHRISTIAN BAPTIST".

1824 A.D.   ALEXANDER CAMPBELL AND BARTON W.
STONE MEET. CAMPBELL HAD LEFT THE
PRESBYTERIAN CHURCH AND BECOME
A PREACHER IN THE REFORMED
BAPTIST CHURCH. STONE ALSO HAD
BEEN PERSECUTED BY ORGANIZATIONS
THAT WANTED HIM TO FOLLOW THEIR
CREEDS INSTEAD OF THE BIBLE.

1825 A.D.   JAMES MONROE, FIFTH PRESIDENT OF
THE UNITED STATES, SAYS IN A SPEECH,
WHILE TALKING OF GOD'S OVERRULING
PROVIDENCE, "EXCEPT THE LORD KEEP
THE CITY, THE WATCHMAN WAKETH IN
VAIN..."

1826 A.D.   BARTON STONE BEGINS PUBLISHING
THE "CHRISTIAN MESSENGER".

1827-1829 A.D.   WALTER SCOTT HOLDS MEETINGS
ACROSS THE WESTERN RESERVE AND
SPARKS A REVIVAL THAT MOVES MANY

	TO BECOME CHRISTIANS BASING THEIR RELIGION ON THE BIBLE ONLY.
1829 A.D.	THE SIXTY-SIXTH YEAR OF JUBILEE.
1830-1837 A.D.	WILLIAM IV, THIRD SON OF GEORGE III, RULES ENGLAND.
1830 A.D.	ALEXANDER CAMBELL BECOMES EDITOR OF THE "MILLENNIUM HARBINGER."
1830-1872 A.D.	SIR CHARLES LYELL BART PUBLISHES ELEVEN EDITIONS OF "PRINCIPLES OF GEOLOGY." HE TAKES THE UNIFORMTARIAN POSITION WHICH GREATLY INFLUENCES CHARLES DARWIN.
1832 A.D.	WALTER SCOTT BEGINS PUBLISHING "THE EVANGELIST."
1837-1901 A.D.	VICTORIA, LAST OF THE HOUSE OF HANOVER, RULES ENGLAND.
1837 A.D.	LEOPOLD VON BUCH COINS THE TERM, "UNIFORMITARIANISM," FOR THE VIEW IN GEOLOGY THAT DENIES THE CATASTROPHE THAT CAME WITH NOAH'S FLOOD.
1840 A.D.	AN EARTH QUAKE ON MOUNT ARARAT APPEARS TO HAVE BROKEN NOAH'S ARK IN HALF, LETTING THE STERN DROP A THOUSAND FEET OR MORE DOWN THE MOUNTAIN SIDE.
1841 A.D.	WILLIAM HENRY HARRISON, THE NINTH PRESIDENT OF THE UNITED STATES, STATES, "SOUND MORALS, RELIGIOUS LIBERTY, AND A JUST SENSE OF RELIGIOUS RESPONSIBILITY ARE ESSENTIALLY CONNECTED WITH ALL TRUE AND LASTING HAPPINESS..."
1845 A.D.	ANDREW JACKSON, THE SEVENTH PRESIDENT OF THE UNITED STATES AND FOUNDER OF THE DEMOCRATIC PARTY, AND RELATIVE OF THE SINGLETONS, WROTE IN HIS WILL, "THE BIBLE IS

TRUE. UPON THAT SACRED VOLUME I REST MY HOPE OF ETERNAL SALVATION THROUGH THE MERITS OF OUR BLESSED LORD AND SAVIOR, JESUS CHRIST..." JAMES KNOX POLK, THE ELEVENTH PRESIDENT OF THE UNITED STATES, DECLARES," I FERVENTLY INVOKE THE AID OF THAT ALMIGHTY RULER OF THE UNIVERSE IN WHOSE HANDS ARE THE DESTINIES OF NATIONS..."

1849 A.D.
ZACHARY TAYLOR, THE TWELFTH PRESIDENT OF THE UNITED STATES, SPEAKING OF THE BIBLE, WROTE, "IT WAS FOR THE LOVE OF TRUTHS OF THIS GREAT BOOK THAT OUR FATHERS ABANDONED THEIR NATIVE SHORES FOR THE WILDERNESS. ANIMATED BY LOFTY PRINCIPLES, THEY TOILED AND SUFFERED TILL THE DESERT BLOSSOMED AS A ROSE..."

c1852 A.D.
JAMES ABRAM GARFIELD, LATER TO BE THE TWENTIETH PRESIDENT OF THE UNITED STATES, SAYS, "IT IS A HABIT OF MINE TO READ A CHAPTER IN THE BIBLE EVERY EVENING..."

1853 A.D.
FRANKLIN PIERCE, THE FOURTEENTH PRESIDENT OF THE UNITED STATES, ACKNOWLEDGED HIS "DEPENDENCE UPON GOD AND HIS OVERRULING PROVIDENCE..."

1858 A.D.
CHARLES DARWIN PRESENTS THE THEORY OF EVOLUTION IN "ON THE ORIGIN OF SPECIES." THIS BECOMES THE RELIGION OF MANY WHO WANT TO DENY THE AUTHORITY OF GOD, OR THE GOD GIVEN RIGHTS AND DIGNITY OF MAN.

CHAPTER TEN
A CHRISTIAN CHRONOLOGY OF HISTORY
(1858 A.D. – 1917A.D.)
A TIME LINE OF HUMAN HISTORY
FROM A CHRISTIAN PROSPECTIVE
Compiled by "God's Friend"

1861 A.D.	ABRAHAM LINCOLN, THE SIXTEENTH PRESIDENT OF THE UNITED STARES, DECLARES, "IT IS FIT AND BECOMING IN ALL PEOPLE, AT ALL TIMES, TO ACKNOWLEDGE AND REVERE THE SUPREME GOVERNMENT OF GOD..."
1861-1865 A.D.	THE AMERICAN CIVIL WAR IS FOUGHT OVER STATES' RIGHTS. ALMOST 700,000 AMERICANS LOOSE THEIR LIVES.
1862 A.D.	MARTIN VAN BUREN, EIGHTH PRESIDENT OF THE UNITED STATES, STATED, DURING HIS FINAL ILLNESS, "THE ATONEMENT OF JESUS CHRIST IS THE ONLY REMEDY AND REST FOR MY SOUL..."
1862 A.D.	LINCOLN PROCLAIMS SLAVES IN SECEDED STATES FREE. THIS IS A POLITICAL MOVE THAT EVENTUALLY LEADS TO THE FREEING OF ALL SLAVE IN THE UNITED STATE. HE ALSO IS BAPTIZED INTO THE CHURCH OF CHRIST. HE IS BAPTIZED BY A PREACHER IN THE MOVEMENT THAT HAD BEEN PARTIALLY FORMED BY STONE, SCOTT, AND CAMBELL, THE RESTORATION MOVEMENT. ABOUT THIS TIME

ANDREW JOHNSON, THE SEVENTEENTH
PRESIDENT OF THE UNITED STATE
AND LINCOLN'S VICE PRESIDENT,
STATES, '...OUR MOTTO: "LIBERTY AND
UNION, ONE AND INSEPARABLE, NOW
AND FOREVER... CHRIST FIRST, OUR
COUNTRY NEXT!"'

1865 A.D.   THE THIRTEENTH AMENDMENT TO
THE CONSTITUTION, IS PASSED AFTER
LINCOLN'S DEATH. IT ENDS SLAVERY IN
THE U.S.A.

1866 A.D.   DAVID LIPSCOMB, A RESTORATION
PREACHER, REVIVES THE "GOSPEL
ADVOCATE" (IT IS STILL A MAJOR
CHRISTIAN PUBLICATION TODAY). IN IT
HE TEACHES THERE ARE THREE IDEAS
OF THE RELATION OF THE CHURCH TO
WORLD POWERS:

1) THE CHURCH SHOULD FORM
ALLIANCES WITH WORLD POWERS
AND USE THEM.

2) POLITICAL GOVERNMENTS ARE OF
DIVINE ORIGIN AND SHOULD BE
SUSTAINED BY THE CHURCH.

3) THE CHURCH AND THE CIVIL
GOVERNMENTS ARE TWO SEPARATE
AND DISTINCT SYSTEMS. THE
CHURCH IS PERFECT AND NEEDS NO
HUMAN HELP. GOD ALLOWS THOSE
WHO REFUSE TO SUBMIT TO THE
DIVINE GOVERNMENT TO FORM
GOVERNMENTS OF THEIR OWN.
WHILE THE CHRISTIAN IS TO HAVE
NO PART IN THIS GOVERNMENT, HE
WILL QUIETLY SUBMIT TO IT WHERE
ITS LAWS DO NOT CONFLICT WITH

THAT OF THE CHURCH.

VIEW 3 WAS SUPPORTED BY LIPSCOMB AND BECAME WIDELY ACCEPTED, ESPECIALLY IN THE SOUTH FOLLOWING THE CIVIL WAR. I BELIEVE THIS TEACHING TO BE TRAGIC AND TO BE BLAMED FOR THE CURRENT LACK OF POLITICAL INPUT OF THE CHURCHES OF CHRIST. THEY ARE A POLITICAL GIANT BARELY BEGINNING TO WAKE UP. OUR SOCIETY SUFFERS BECAUSE IT HAS BEEN DENIED THEIR GOD TRAINED WISDOM AND DIRECTION. (THAT IS NOT TO SAY MEN LIKE GEORGE HOUSE, FORMER STATE OF CALIFORNIA CONGRESSMAN AND SPECIAL PROSECUTOR KEN STARR, BOTH PRODUCTS OF THE RESTORATION MOVEMENT CHURCHES OF CHRIST, HAVE NOT HAD THEIR IMPACT ON U.S. POLITICS). MANY HONORABLE MEN WITH GREAT MENTAL ABILITY WITHIN THE RESTORATION MOVEMENT HAVE PURPOSEFULLY AVOIDED SECULAR POLITICAL INVOLVEMENT. A MANY TIMES GREAT GRANDFATHER OF MINE (JOHN ADAMS) HELPED SHAPE THIS NATION SO THAT CHRIST AND HIS FOLLOWERS WOULD HAVE A PLACE UNDER THE SUN THAT WELCOMED THEIR PARTICIPATION IN   SECULAR GOVERNMENTS.
IF CHRISTIANS CAN GIVE TO THEIR FAMILY AND NEIGHBORS A BETTER, MORE FREE PLACE TO LIVE, WHERE EXPRESSING THE LOVE OF JESUS IN YOUR LIFE IS NOT A CRIME, THEN THEY SHOULD CHERISH THAT OPPORTUNITY

TO PARTICIPATE IN IMPERFECT
SECULAR GOVERNMENT. THE GREED
FOR POWER AND AUTHORITY HAS
USUALLY RESULTED IN GOVERNMENTS
RESENTING THE SUPERIOR PLACE OF
GOD'S GOVERNMENT IN HUMAN LIVES,
RESULTING IN ALMOST UNBEARABLE
PERSECUTION FOR THOSE WHO
ORDERED THEIR LIVES CORRECTLY.
LET US GIVE TO GOD WHAT IS GOD'S
AND TO CAESAR WHAT IS CAESAR'S.
IF CAESAR IS REASONABLE, EXERCISE
YOUR INFLUENCE IN THE AFFAIRS
OF CAESAR SO THAT YOU CAN DO
YOUR GIVING IN AN ATMOSPHERE
OF PEACE AND HARMONY. IF IT BE
POSSIBLE, AS MUCH AS LIETH IN US,
WE MUST LIVE PEACEABLY WITH ALL
MEN. THROUGH OUR INFLUENCE OF
CAESAR WE MAKE THE KEEPING OF THIS
COMMANDMENT POSSIBLE AND AVOID
MUCH SORROW. IN PASSING LET IT
ALSO BE NOTED THAT THE PERFECTLY
ORGANIZED GOVERNMENT OF GOD
LOVED US AND LET US PARTICIPATE.
OUR IMPERFECTIONS AND REBELLIONS
AGAINST CHRIST, HAVE AT TIMES, MADE
THAT GOVERNMENT MISERABLE TO
LIVE UNDER AND THE JUST RECIPIENT
OF CHRISTIAN RESISTANCE AS
CHRISTIANS ANSWERED TO THE HEAD
AND NOT TO IMPERFECT, ARROGANT
OFFICIALS. THE NUREMBERG
TRIALS STAND AS A GREAT SECULAR
DECLARATION OF THIS REQUIREMENT
TO ANSWER TO GOD ABOVE HUMAN
COMMANDS.

1867 A.D.   CANADA BECOMES A SELF GOVERNING
NATION OF THE BRITISH EMPIRE.

1868 A.D.	JAMES BUCHANAN, THE FIFTEENTH PRESIDENT OF THE UNITED STATES, WRITES TO HIS BROTHER, "I TRUST IN GOD THAT, THROUGH THE MERITS AND ATONEMENT OF HIS SON, WE MAY BOTH BE PREPARED FOR THE INEVITABLE CHANGE."
1871 A.D.	KING WILLIAM I OF PRUSSIA UNITES THE GERMAN STATES AND BECOMES GERMAN KAISER (EMPEROR).
1874 A.D.	R. M. BISHOP, AN ELDER OF A RESTORATION MOVEMENT CONGREGATION IN CINCINNATI, IS ELECTED GOVERNOR OF OHIO.
1876 A.D.	ULYSSES S. GRANT, THE EIGHTEENTH PRESIDENT OF THE UNITED STATES, WRITES, "HOLD FAST TO THE BIBLE AS THE SHEET ANCHOR OF YOUR LIBERTIES; WRITE ITS PRECEPTS IN YOUR HEARTS, AND PRACTICE THEM IN YOUR LIVES." SIR JAMES BRINGS BACK TO LONDON A PIECE OF NOAH'S ARK FROM MOUNT ARARAT.
1877 A.D.	RUTHERFORD BIRCHARD HAYES, THE NINETEENTH PRESIDENT OF THE UNITED STATES, DECLARES, "I BELIEVE ALSO IN THE HOLY SCRIPTURES AS THE REVEALED WORD OF GOD TO THE WORLD FOR ITS ENLIGHTENMENT AND SALVATION."
1880 A.D.	JAMES ABRAM GARFIELD, A PREACHER IN THE RESTORATION MOVEMENT, IS ELECTED PRESIDENT OF THE UNITED STATES. R. M. GANO OF DALLAS, A PROMINENT RESTORATION PREACHER, IS URGED BY THE "GREENBACKERS" TO RUN FOR GOVERNOR OF TEXAS. GANO REFUSED. THE "CHRISTIAN PREACHER" WROTE, "BROTHER GANO

COULD DO MORE GOOD PREACHING
THE GOSPEL THAN TEN CONGRESSMEN
COULD MAKING LAWS, EVEN IF THEY
ALWAYS MADE GOOD ONES. THE
GOSPEL OF CHRIST IS SUPERIOR
TO THE GREENBACK GOSPEL..."
SIMILARLY O. A. BURGESS, ANOTHER
RESTORATION PREACHER IS URGED TO
RUN ON THE REPUBLICAN TICKET FOR
GOVERNOR OF INDIANA, BUT REFUSES.
RESTORATION PREACHERS WHO RAN
FOR OFFICE, BUT WERE DEFEATED
INCLUDED D. R. DUNGAN, A CANDIDATE
FOR GOVERNOR OF IOWA, AND J.M.
PICKENS, A CANDIDATE FOR GOVERNOR
OF ALABAMA.
SIR CHARLES LYELL BART PUBLISHES
THE STATEMENT, "NO CAUSES
WHATEVER HAVE FROM THE EARLIEST
TIME TO WHICH WE CAN LOOK BACK,
TO THE PRESENT, EVER ACTED BUT
THOSE NOW ACTING AND THAT THEY
NEVER ACTED WITH DIFFERENT
DEGREES OF ENERGY FROM THAT
WHICH THEY NOW EXERT." THIS
STATEMENT BECOMES A CENTRAL
PRINCIPLE OF THE EVOLUTIONARY
THEORY. IT DENIES NOAH'S FLOOD.

1881-1885 A.D. CHESTER ALAN ARTHUR, THE SON
OF A BAPTIST PREACHER, BECOMES
THE TWENTY-FIRST PRESIDENT OF
THE UNITED STATES. HE EARNED THE
NICKNAME, "GENTLEMAN BOSS", FOR
HIS SUCCESS IN RUNNING AN HONEST
GOVERNMENT.

1882 A.D. REFLECTING ON HIS EARLIER WORK,
CHARLES DARWIN COMMENTED, "I
WAS A YOUNG MAN WITH UNFORMED
IDEAS. I THREW OUT QUERIES,

	SUGGESTIONS, WONDERING ALL THE TIME OVER EVERYTHING; AND TO MY ASTONISHMENT THE IDEAS TOOK LIKE WILDFIRE. PEOPLE MADE A RELIGION OF THEM."
1883 A.D.	TURKISH COMMISSION SEES AND REPORTS THE PRESENCE OF NOAH'S ARK ON ARARAT.
1884 A.D.	A. MCGARY BEGINS PUBLISHING THE "FIRM FOUNDATION," A CURRENT GOSPEL PUBLICATION WITH A DEDICATED FOLLOWING. HIS FATHER HAD FOUGHT WITH SAM HOUSTON'S POORLY EQUIPPED AND GREATLY OUT NUMBERED ARMY AGAINST SANTA ANNA. WHEN HOUSTON'S ARMY SUDDENLY TURNED AND DEFEATED THE MEXICAN ARMY, A. MCGARY'S FATHER HAD BEEN THE ONE THAT GUARDED THE BEDRAGGLED MEXICAN CAPTIVE THAT TURN OUT TO BE SANTA ANNA. MCGARY GREW UP PLAYING WITH SAM HOUSTON'S CHILDREN. WHEN MCGARY RETURNED FROM THE CIVIL WAR HIS FATHER'S HOMESTEAD HAD BEEN PILLAGED BY UNION SOLDIERS. WHEN HE PASSED SOME UNION SOLDIERS ON A ROAD, HE SAW THEY WERE RIDING HIS FATHER'S HORSES. HE PULLED A GUN AND TOOK THEM BACK. HE LATER BECAME SHERIFF OF MADISON COUNTY. HE WAS KNOWN FOR BOLD, FEARLESS ACTIONS. WHEN CHALLENGED BY THE KU-KLUX KLAN, HE BOLDLY ANNOUNCED THAT, "YOU KNOW WHERE I LIVE, MY DOOR IS ALWAYS UNLOCKED, YOU CAN COME ANY TIME, BUT YOU BETTER BRING A WHEELBARROW TO CARRY

YOUR BOYS HOME IN."
HE BECAME A RESTORATION GOSPEL
PREACHER, BUT HIS SERMONS AS
WELL AS HIS PUBLICATIONS FIT HIS
CHARACTER.

1885 A.D.   STEPHEN GROVER CLEVELAND, THE
TWENTY SECOND AND TWENTY
FOURTH PRESIDENT OF THE UNITED
STATES URGED, "LET US NOT TRUST
TO HUMAN EFFORT ALONE, BUT
HUMBLY ACKNOWLEDGE THE POWER
AND GOODNESS OF ALMIGHTY GOD
WHO PRESIDES OVER THE DESTINY OF
NATIONS, AND WHO HAS AT ALL TIMES
BEEN REVEALED IN OUR COUNTRY'S
HISTORY."

1887 A.D.   PRINCE NURIE OF BABYLON SEES
NOAH'S ARK.

c1890 A.D.   BENJAMIN HARRISON, THE TWENTY
THIRD PRESIDENT OF THE UNITED
STATES, WROTE, "IT IS A GREAT
COMFORT TO TRUST GOD ..."

1892 A.D.   IRA J. CHASE, A RESTORATION GOSPEL
PREACHER, BECOMES GOVERNOR
OF INDIANA. IN A SUPREME COURT
DECISION, (CHURCH OF THE HOLY
TRINITY VS. UNITED STATES), THE
U.S. SUPREME COURT STATES," OUR
LAWS AND OUR INSTITUTIONS MUST
NECESSARILY BE BASED UPON AND
EMBODY THE TEACHINGS OF THE
REDEEMER OF MANKIND..."

1897 A.D.   WILLIAM MCKINLEY, THE TWENTY
FIFTH PRESIDENT OF THE UNITED
STATES, STATES OF THE BIBLE, "THE
MORE CLOSELY WE OBSERVE ITS DIVINE
PRECEPTS, THE BETTER CITIZENS WE
WILL BECOME AND THE HIGHER WILL
BE OUR DESTINY AS A NATION."

1901-1910A.D.	EDWARD VII, SON OF VICTORIA, RULES ENGLAND.
1902A.D.	GEORGE HERROPEAN VISITS THE ARK AND CLIMBS ON IT.
c1903 A.D.	THEODORE ROOSEVELT, THE TWENTY SIXTH PRESIDENT OF THE UNITED STATES, DECLARES, "A THOROUGH KNOWLEDGE OF THE BIBLE IS WORTH MORE THAN A COLLEGE EDUCATION."
1907 A.D.	"STEALTH BANKERS" CREATE THE FEDERAL RESERVE TO CONTROL THE U.S. MONEY SUPPLY.
1909 A.D.	W. H. TAFT, THE 27TH PRESIDENT OF THE UNITED STATES, PUBLICLY ASKED FOR THE "AID OF ALMIGHTY GOD" IN THE PERFORMANCE OF HIS JOB.
1910-1936 A.D.	GEORGE V, SECOND SON OF EDWARD VII, FIRST OF THE HOUSE OF WINDSOR, RULES ENGLAND.
1912-1915A.D.	ALFRED WEGENER PRESENTS AN EVOLUTION SUPPORTIVE THEORY OF CONTINENTAL DRIFT THAT ENDED UP BEING REJECTED AT THAT TIME. THOSE WHO TRUSTED IN HIS LOGIC STAGED A GOLD RUSH TO SOUTH AMERICA, BUT FOUND NO GOLD. THE MINERAL DEPOSITS OF AFRICA AND SOUTH AMERICA PROVED TO BE DIFFERENT.
c1913 A.D.	WOODROW WILSON, THE TWENTY EIGHTH PRESIDENT OF THE UNITED STATES, ASSERTS, "A MAN HAS DEPRIVED HIMSELF OF THE BEST THERE IS IN THE WORLD WHO HAS DEPRIVED HIMSELF OF THIS, A KNOWLEDGE OF THE BIBLE."
1914-1920 A.D.	AUSTRIA, SUPPORTED BY GERMANY, BEGINS WORLD WAR I. ALLIED FORCES ARE ENGLAND, FRANCE, RUSSIA, BELGIUM, SERBIA, MONTENEGRO, GREECE, ITALY, AND THE UNITED

STATES. THE OPPOSING CENTRAL POWERS ARE GERMANY, AUSTRIA-HUNGARY, BULGARIA, AND TURKEY. BEFORE THE END OF 1915, SERBIA AND MONTENEGRO FALL. ITALY DID NOT ENTER THE CONFLICT UNTIL MID 1915. GREECE AND THE UNITED STATES DID NOT ENTER UNTIL 1917. THE RUSSIAN REVOLUTION ELIMINATED RUSSIA AS A USEFUL ALLY BEFORE THE U.S. ENTERED THE WAR.

10, 000,000 ARE KILLED AND 20,000,000 ARE WOUNDED. MOST OF THE CASUALTIES WERE FROM EUROPEAN NATIONS. 1915, 1916, 1918, RUSSIAN AVIATORS SEE NOAH'S ARK, AND THEN THEIR ARMY VISITS IT EACH YEAR MAPPING AND PHOTOGRAPHING THE ARK

1917 A.D.   COMMUNIST REVOLUTION BEGINS IN RUSSIA. THEY DENY THE EXISTENCE OF GOD AND GOD GIVEN RIGHTS AND HUMAN DIGNITY. THE STATE IS VIEWED AS HAVING ULTIMATE AUTHORITY. THE RELIGION IS ATHEISTIC EVOLUTION AND THERE IS TREMENDOUS PERSECUTION FOR PRACTICING CHRISTIANS. THE STATE TRIES TO TAKE THE BIBLE AWAY FROM THE PEOPLE. THE RELIGION OF EVOLUTION IS USED AS THE FOUNDATION FOR ITS FIRST GOVERNMENTAL EXPERIMENT.

CHAPTER ELEVEN
A CHRISTIAN CHRONOLOGY OF HISTORY
(1917 A.D. – 1953 A.D.)
A TIME LINE OF HUMAN HISTORY
FROM A CHRISTIAN PROSPECTIVE
Compiled by "God's Friend"

1917-1924 A.D.	IN ORDER TO SECURE CONTROL OVER THE LIVES OF THE PEOPLE OF THE SOVIET UNION, THE COMMUNIST PARTY KILLS 62,000,000 SOVIET CITIZENS.
1917-1924 A.D.	LENIN RULES THE SOVIET UNION.
1918 A.D.	ALLENBY DEFEATS THE OTTOMANS AT MEGIDDO.
1921 A.D.	WARREN GAMALIEL HARDING, THE TWENTY NINTH PRESIDENT OF THE UNITED STATES, ANNOUNCES, "I HAVE ALWAYS BELIEVED IN THE INSPIRATION OF HOLY SCRIPTURES."
1923-1929 A.D.	THE SOVIET UNION, UNDER COMMUNISM, EXPERIENCES WIDE SPREAD CIVIL WAR AND FAMINE.
1924-1938 A.D.	STALIN BEGINS SHARING CONTROL OF THE SOVIET UNION WITH SEVEN COMRADES. FIVE ARE EXECUTED AND ONE IS EXILED, LEAVING STALIN IN CONTROL. THIS GODLESS FAITH SYSTEM SPREADS RUTHLESSNESS AMONG FRIENDS. YOU CAN TRACE ITS BETRAYALS BY THE CORPSES.
1925 A.D.	A TENNESSEE LAW FORBIDS THE TEACHING OF EVOLUTION IN THE PUBLIC SCHOOLS. JOHN THOMAS

	SCOPES, A SCIENCE TEACHER, VIOLATES THE LAW. ABOUT THE ONLY TESTIMONY HEARD BY THE JURY IS THE TESTIMONY OF TWO STUDENTS WHO SAY HE TAUGHT EVOLUTION. THE DEFENSE DOES PRESENT INFORMATION ABOUT "NABRASKA MAN" OUTSIDE THE HEARING OF THE JURY. SCOPES IS FOUND GUILTY. "THE NEBRASKA MAN" IS LATER FOUND TO BE A FRAUD. SINCE THEN ADVOCATES FOR EVOLUTION AND THEIR SPIN DOCTORS HAVE GROSSLY MISREPRESENTED THE CASE.
c1926 A.D.	JOHN CALVIN COOLIDGE, THE THIRTIETH PRESIDENT OF THE UNITED STATES, POINTS OUT THAT, "THE FOUNDATIONS OF OUR SOCIETY AND OUR GOVERNMENT REST SO MUCH ON THE TEACHINGS OF THE BIBLE, THAT IT WOULD BE DIFFICULT TO SUPPORT THEM IF FAITH IN THESE TEACHINGS WOULD CEASE TO BE PRACTICALLY UNIVERSAL IN OUR COUNTRY ..."
1929 A.D.	THE SIXTY-EIGHTH YEAR OF JUBILEE.
1929-1932 A.D.	THERE IS AN ECONOMIC CRASH IN THE UNITED STATES.
1932 A.D.	MAO LEADS IN THE CREATION OF CHINESE COMMUNIST REPUBLIC OF JIANGXI. A UKRAINE FAMINE KILLS 3,000,000. THE SOVIET UNION PUTS MILLIONS IN PENAL COLONIES AND USES THEM AS SLAVE LABOR.
1933 A.D.	THE NAZI PARTY COMES TO POWER IN GERMANY. THEY BELIEVE IN THE THEORY OF EVOLUTION. THEY JUSTIFY ARYAN RACIAL DOMINANCE AND UTILIZATION OF OTHER RACES

	AS CATTLE. THE CONCEPT OF GOD GIVEN RIGHTS AND DIGNITY FOR NON – ARYANS IS REJECTED. NATURAL SELECTION MEANS THEY ARE DESTINED TO RULE AND OTHERS SERVE OR BECOME EXTINCT.
1934 A.D.	CHIANG KAI- SHEK LEADS A CHINESE NATIONALIST ARMY THAT FORCES THE COMMUNIST OUT OF THE JIANGXI AREA. 100, 000 COMMUNIST RELOCATE TO SHAANXI PROVINCE.
1935 A.D.	FRANKLIN D. ROOSEVELT, THE 32ND PRESIDENT OF THE UNITED STATES, DECLARES, 'WE CANNOT READ THE HISTORY OF OUR RISE AND DEVELOPMENT AS A NATION, WITHOUT RECKONING WITH THE PLACE THE BIBLE HAS OCCUPIED IN SHAPING THE ADVANCES OF THE REPUBLIC … WHERE WE HAVE BEEN THE TRUEST AND MOST CONSISTENT IN OBEYING ITS PRECEPTS, WE HAVE ATTAINED THE GREATEST MEASURE OF CONTENTMENT AND PROSPERITY …"
1936-1938 A.D.	GERMANY TAKES THE RHINELAND, AUSTRIA, CZECHOSLOVAKIA. GEORGE VI, SECOND SON OF GEORGE V, RULES ENGLAND.
1937 A.D.	JAPAN ATTACKS CHINA. THE NATIONALIST AND THE COMMUNIST CHINESE AGREE TO JOIN AND FIGHT THE JAPANESE.
1938-1955 A.D.	STALIN RUTHLESSLY RULES THE SOVIET UNION.
1929 A.D.	STALIN AND HITLER AGREE TO DIVIDE POLAND. RUSSIA IS GIVEN HALF OF POLAND, ESTONIA, LATVIA, AND LITHUAINIA. GERMANY INVADES

POLAND, RUSSIA INVADES FINLAND, AND WORLD WAR II BEGINS.

1939-1945 A.D.   NAZI CONCENTRATION CAMPS KILL 12,000,000 CIVILIANS. MANY JEWS AND CHRISTIANS, WHO RESIST THE NAZI BELIEF SYSTEM, DIE. MOST OF THE MEMBERS OF THE CHURCHES OF CHRIST IN EASTERN EUROPE ARE EXTERMINATED. MORE DIE IN THE CONCENTRATION CAMPS OF WORLD WAR II THAN DIED ON THE BATTLE FIELDS OF WORLD WAR I. THE NAZI BELIEF SYSTEM IS AN EVIL MOVEMENT GROWING FROM THE ATHEISTIC THEORY OF EVOLUTION. MEN ARE VIEWED AS A DEVELOPING SPECIES OF ANIMALS. THE ARIAN RACE IS VIEWED AS THE GREATEST ACHIEVEMENT OF EVOLUTION WITH THE REST OF MANKIND FOR THEIR USE AS OTHERS USE FARM ANIMALS. FOR GERMANS TO BECOME WORLD RULERS IS MERELY A FULFILLMENT OF DESTINY.

1940 A.D   FRANCE SURRENDERS TO GERMANY.

1941 A.D.   GERMANY INVADES RUSSIA, PROVING THERE IS NO HONOR AMONG THIEVES. RUSSIA SWITCHES SIDES.

1942 A.D.   U.S. SCIENTISTS CREATE THE FIRST CONTROLLED CHAIN REACTION.

1943 A.D.   HERBERT HOOVER, THE 31 ST. PRESIDENT OF THE UNITED STATES ISSUED A JOINT STATEMENT WITH THE WIVES OF THE 30TH, THE 27TH, THE 26TH, THE 23RD, AND THE 22ND PRESIDENTS OF THE UNITED STATES, (AND OTHER LEADERS), WHICH AFFIRMED THAT, "DEMOCRACY IS THE OUTGROWTH OF THE RELIGIOUS CONVICTION OF THE SACREDNESS OF EVERY HUMAN LIFE.

	ON THE RELIGIOUS SIDE, ITS HIGHEST EMBODIMENT IS THE BIBLE, ON THE POLITICAL SIDE, THE CONSTITUTION".
1944 A.D.	WESTERN NATIONS AGREE TO A CURRENCY PEGGING SYSTEM, AT BRETTON WOODS, NEW HAMPSHIRE. THIS ESTABLISHES A VALUE FOR MAJOR CURRENCIES AGAINST THE US DOLLAR, WHICH IN TURN IS PEGGED AT $35.00 TO THE TROY OUNCE OF GOLD. THIS IS KNOWN AS THE GOLD STANDARD.
1945 A.D.	THE U.S. TESTS THE FIRST ATOMIC BOMB, AND THEN DROPS TWO BOMBS ON JAPAN. WORLD WAR II ENDS WITH THE SURRENDER OF JAPAN AND GERMANY.
1947-1950 A.D	MAO PROCLAIMS THE PEOPLE'S REPUBLIC OF CHINA, AND FIGHTS AGAINST FORCES UNDER CHIANG KAI-SHEK. MAIN LAND CHINA FALLS UNDER COMMUNIST RULE. CHIANG KIA-SHEK IS FORCED TO FALL BACK TO FORMOSA WHERE HIS PEOPLE ESTABLISH NATIONALIST CHINA OR TAIWAN.
1948A.D	THE ESTABLISHMENT OF A NEW JEWISH NATION OF ISRAEL LEADS TO THE FIRST ARAB-ISRAELI WAR. WESTERN POWERS DESIRE TO GIVE THE JEWS THEIR OWN LAND, BUT PALESTINIAN ARABS ALREADY CLAIM THE REGION. THE ISRAELIS DEFEAT ARAB FORCES AT ZARIN, MEGIDDO, MISHMAR, HAEMEK, AND LEJJUN. TITO BREAKS WITH THE SOVIET UNION, BUT CZECHOSLOVAKIA REMAINS COMMUNIST.
1950-2000+ A.D.	THE COMMUNIST PARTY OF CHINA RULES WITH AN IRON HAND, KILLING OVER 38,000,000 PEOPLE TO STAY IN CONTROL. THEIR GREED FOR POWER

COSTS MORE LIVES THAN MOST ANY
OTHER RUTHLESS HUMAN EFFORT IN
HISTORY, AND IS ONLY SURPASSED BY
THE RUTHLESS COMMUNIST EFFORT
FOR CONTROL OF THE SOVIET UNION.
THEY ESTABLISH SLAVE LABOR CAMPS,
TRY TO BAND THE BIBLE, AND SELL
PRISONER BODY PARTS. THEIR EFFORT
TO BAND THE BIBLE FAILS, AND HOUSE
CHURCHES SPRING UP THROUGH
OUT THEIR EMPIRE. THEY THEN
TRY TO CONTROL CHRISTIANITY BY
OUTLAWING SERVICES THAT ARE NOT
HELD IN PUBLIC FACILITIES. THEY
ESTABLISH A GOVERNMENT AGENCY TO
APPOINT THE PREACHERS PERMITTED
TO PREACH AT THE PERMITTED
SERVICES. THE PREACHERS ARE
NORMALLY UNBELIEVERS, MEMBERS
OF THE COMMUNIST PARTY. THEY
ALSO DENY GOVERNMENT SERVICES
(HOUSING, MEDICAL CARE, AND FOOD)
TO FAMILIES WITH MORE THAN ONE
CHILD. SINCE IT IS CUSTOM FOR THE
SON TO STAY WITH HIS PARENTS AND
HELP THEM IN THEIR OLD AGE, AND
THE DAUGHTER TO LEAVE HER HOME
AND HELP HER HUSBAND'S PARENTS,
A GREAT IMBALANCE OF YOUNG MEN
DEVELOPS.

c1950 A.D.   HANS GRIMM, A SURVIVOR OF
THE GERMAN CONCENTRATION
CAMPS, A NON-CATHOLIC, NON-
GREEK ORTHODOX MEMBER OF THE
CHURCHES OF CHRIST OF EASTERN
EUROPE, WRITES A HISTORY OF HIS
PEOPLE. THEIR TRADITIONS AND
ORIGINS WENT BACK TO THE TIME
BEFORE CONSTANTINE. HE WAS

DELIGHTED TO DISCOVER THAT THE RESTORATION MOVEMENT ON THE AMERICAN WESTERN FRONTIER HAD PRODUCED THE SAME, IDENTICAL BELIEF SYSTEM AND FELLOWSHIP IN AMERICA. HIS INITIAL CONTACT WITH THE AMERICAN CHURCHES OF CHRIST CAME THROUGH OTTIS GATEWOOD, AN ORGANIZER OF THE COLD WAR BIBLE PRINTING AND SMUGGLING RING IN CZECHOSLOVAKIA.

1950-1953 A.D.   NORTH KOREA, BACKED BY COMMUNIST CHINA, INVADES SOUTH KOREA. UNITED NATIONS FORCES, LED BY U.S. FORCES, DRIVES THEM OUT OF SOUTH KOREA. GEN. MACARHTUR WANTS TO INVADE RED CHINA, BUT PRESIDENT TRUMAN FIRES HIM INSTEAD.

CHAPTER TWELVE
A CHRISTIAN CHRONOLOGY OF HISTORY
(1953 A.D. – 1997 A.D.)
A TIME LINE OF HUMAN HISTORY
FROM A CHRISTIAN PROSPECTIVE
Compiled by "God's Friend"

1952 A.D.	QUEEN ELIZABETH II ASCENDS TO THE THROWN OF ENGLAND WITH FIRST WIDESPREAD USE OF TELEVISION.
c1953 A.D.	HARRY S. TRUMAN, 33RD PRESIDENT OF THE UNITED STATES, ADMONISHES, "THE FUNDAMENTAL BASIS OF THIS NATION'S LAWS WERE GIVEN BY MOSES ON THE MOUNT. THE FUNDAMENTAL BASIS OF OUR BILL OF RIGHTS COMES FROM THE TEACHINGS WE GET FROM EXODUS AND ST. MATTHEW, FROM ISAIAH AND ST. PAUL. I DON'T THINK WE EMPHASIZE THAT ENOUGH THESE DAYS. IF WE DON'T HAVE A PROPER FUNDAMENTAL MORAL BACKGROUND, WE WILL FINALLY END UP WITH A TOTALITARIAN GOVERNMENT WHICH DOES NOT BELIEVE IN RIGHTS FOR ANYBODY EXCEPT THE STATE!"
1953-1961 A.D.	IKE EISENHOWER IS PRESIDENT OF THE UNITED STATES.
1954 A.D.	WITH THE SUPPORT OF PRESIDENT EISENHOWER THE PHRASE, "UNDER GOD," IS ADDED TO THE UNITED STATES PLEDGE OF ALLEGIANCE. CONSISTENT WITH THE DECLARATION

| | OF INDEPENDENCE, THIS RECOGNIZES GOD'S RANK ABOVE THE NATION'S GOVERNMENT. |

1955 A.D. STALIN DIES.

1956-1964 A.D. NIKITA KRUSHCHEV DENOUNCES STALIN AND RULES THE SOVIET UNION. 1956 A.D. PRESIDENT IKE SAYS THE UNITED STATES WILL HELP ENSLAVED PEOPLES THROW OFF COMMUNIST RULE. HUNGARIANS REVOLT. THE U.S. ONLY TALKS. SOVIET TANKS CRUSH A POPULAR REVOLT IN HUNGARY. 7,000 ARE KILLED FIGHTING TANKS WITH STONES AND BOTTLES OF GASOLINE. THOUSANDS BECOME REFUGEES FLEEING TO AUSTRIA. POLISH WORKERS RIOT. ADILI STEVENSON RUNS FOR THE SECOND TIME AGAINST IKE FOR THE PRESIDENCY OF THE UNITED STATES. TO ME HE SEEMED TO BE ONE OF THE BEST CANDIDATES EVER FIELDED BY THE DEMOCRATIC PARTY. HE STATES THAT THERE ARE TWO DANGEROUSLY DISHONEST MEN IN AMERICAN POLITICS, RICHARD NIXON AND JOHN KENNEDY. OF THE TWO HE DECLARES KENNEDY THE MOST DANGEROUS BECAUSE HE IS ALSO RICH.

1957 A.D. A COUP SPONSORED BY RUSSIA PUTS PRO-COMMUNISTS IN CHARGE OF SYRIA. RUSSIA PUTS UP TWO SPUTNIKS AND BEATS THE U.S. INTO SPACE. IN THE U.S., LITTLE ROCK CENTRAL HIGH SCHOOL IS INTEGRATED.

1959 A.D. NIKITA KHRUSHCHEV TOURS THE U.S. HE BOASTS THAT, WITHOUT FIRING A SHOT, COMMUNISM WILL BURY THE U.S., AND BY 1995 WILL MARCH IN AS CONQUERORS. HE SAYS WE WILL

FORGET ABOUT FOREIGN AFFAIRS, AND BECOME SO INVOLVED IN SPORTS THAT WE WILL NOT REALIZE WHAT IS HAPPENING.

1960 A.D. THE SEGUNDO, CA. CHURCH OF CHRIST AND THE STOCKTON, CA. CENTRAL CHURCH OF CHRIST BEGIN AN ETHIOPIAN MISSION OUTREACH. SEGUNDO SUPPORTS THE BOB GOWEN FAMILY AND THE CENTRAL CHURCH SUPPORTS THE CARL THOMPSON FAMILY. EMPEROR HAILE SELASSIE REQUIRES THAT THE CHURCH BUILD A PROGRAM THAT WILL BE OF SERVICE TO HIS COUNTRY. THE CHURCH BEGINS A SCHOOL FOR THE DEAF. THIS SERVICE ENLARGED AND THE CHURCH NOW PROVIDES TRAINING FOR MANY DEAF STUDENTS. THEY RUN ALL THE TRAINING FOR THE DEAF IN ETHIOPIA TO THE CURRENT TIME. A DAUGHTER OF THE EMPEROR GAVE THE CHURCH A 99 YEAR LEASE ON COMPOUNDS FOR THE FIRST DEAF SCHOOL.

1961 A.D. JOHN F. KENNEDY, DURING HIS INAUGURAL ADDRESS, PROCLAIMS, "THE RIGHTS OF MAN COME NOT FROM THE GENEROSITY OF THE STATE, BUT FROM THE HAND OF GOD..."

1961-1963 A.D. KENNEDY IS THE FIRST CATHOLIC PRESIDENT OF THE UNITED STATES. CUBA SLIPS INTO COMMUNIST HANDS. KENNEDY DENIES FREEDOM FORCES PROMISED AIR SUPPORT AT THE BAY OF PIGS AND CUBAN PATRIOTS ARE SLAUGHTERED BY TANKS. AFTER THIS CASTRO THREATENS THAT THE COMMUNISTS WILL BRING THE U.S. DOWN THROUGH DRUGS. KENNEDY

	PROVIDES THE NATION WITH THE FAMOUS QUOTE, "ASK NOT WHAT YOUR COUNTRY CAN DO FOR YOU, BUT WHAT YOU CAN DO FOR YOUR COUNTRY."
1962A.D.	THE THEORY OF CONTINENTAL DRIFT IS REVIVED WITH THE THEORIES OF SEA FLOOR SPREADING AND MAGNETIC REVERSAL. IT IS DISCOVERED THAT THE EARTH IS CRACKED INTO TWENTY-ONE PLATI AND CRACKED DOWN THE MIDDLE OF THE ATLANTIC WITH MAGNETIC STRIPES ON BOTH SIDES OF THE ATLANTIC CRACK. RUSH TO SUPPORT THE THEORY OF EVOLUTION IGNORES THE FACT THAT GEOLOGICAL SURVEYS OF NORTH AMERICAN AND EUROPEAN ROCK FORMATIONS SHOW NO MAGNETIC REVERSALS IN ALL OF GEOLOGICAL TIME . THEY DO SHOW A CATACLYSMIC SKIP IN POLE LOCATIONS ABOUT TWO THIRDS OF THE WAY BACK IN THE MIGRATION RECORD. THE CRUST MOVED SUDDENLY 5,000 MILES TO THE EAST IN RELATIONSHIP TO THE CORE. THIS SUGGESTS AN ACCORDION LIKE FOLDING OF THE ATLANTIC OCEAN BOTTOM CRUST INSTEAD OF MAGNETIC REVERSAL. THE AVERAGE WIDTH OF THE STRIPES IS THE SAME AS THE AVERAGE THICKNESS OF OCEAN BOTTOM CRUST (SEE 2524-2523B.C.).
1962-1973 A.D.	THE UNITED STATS BECOMES INVOLVED IN THE VIETNAM WAR. COMMUNIST NORTH VIETNAM INVADES SOUTH VIETNAM. PRESIDENT KENNEDY BEGINS AMERICAN INVOLVEMENT. PRESIDENT JOHNSON INCREASES INVOLVEMENT. U.S. LEADERS ARE NOT WILLING TO LET AMERICAN OR SOUTH VIETNAM FORCES INVADE THE NORTH TO BRING THE WAR TO A CLOSE. PRESIDENT NIXON,

	PROMISING THE SOUTH VIETNAMESE CONTINUED US ARMS AND SUPPORT, DISENGAGES U.S. TROOPS. AFTER DISENGAGEMENT, CONGRESSMAN CHURCH GETS A LAW PASSED THAT FORBIDS THE USE OF AMERICAN AIR POWER IN SOUTHEAST ASIA.
1963A.D.	PRESIDENT KENNEDY IS ASSASSINATED.
1963-1969 A.D.	L.B. JOHNSON IS PRESIDENT OF THE UNITED STATES.
1964-1982 A.D.	BREZHENEV LEADS THE SOVIET UNION.
1964-1967 A.D.	BILLY CURL WORKS AS AN ETHIOPIAN MISSIONARY SUPPORTED BY THE SAN FRANCISCO UP-TOWN CHURCH OF CHRIST.
1965 A.D.	PRESIDENT JOHNSON QUOTES THE PRAYER OF KING SOLOMON FROM THE BIBLE AND APPLIES IT TO HIMSELF, "GIVE ME NOW WISDOM AND KNOWLEDGE THAT I MAY GO OUT AND COME IN BEFORE THIS PEOPLE."
1967 A.D.	THE ISRAELIS DEFEAT THE ARABS AT THE RAMAT DAVID AIRFIELD...A BATTLE NEAR MEGIDDO.
1967-1974 A.D.	JANE FONDA IS AN AMERICAN LEADER OF THE MOVEMENT TO TURN COUNTRIES OF SOUTHEAST ASIA OVER TO COMMUNISM. SHE PREACHES THE VIRTUES OF NORTH VIETNAM AND EARNS THE NAME, "HANOI JANE."
1968-1971 A.D.	JOHN ED CLARK AND DON LAZZARESCHI BECOME LEADERS IN THE CHURCH OF CHRIST ETHIOPIAN MISSION OUT REACH. A PREACHER SCHOOL IS HELD TO TEACH TWELVE NATIVE PREACHERS FROM THE KAMBATTA AREA. BROTHER BEHAILU, BROTHER EROMO, AND BROTHER ART REED SELECTED THE CANDIDATES.

	BROTHER EROMO AND BROTHER BEHAILU HAD BECOME NATIVE LEADERS IN THE ADDIS ABABA CHURCH. THE OUTREACH HAS OVER 3,000 IN REGULAR ATTENDANCE IN 101 CONGREGATIONS.
1970 A.D.	A MILITARY COUP FRIENDLY TO SOUTH VIETNAM AND THE U.S. TAKES PLACE IN CAMBODIA. THE CAMBODIAN KING, NORODOM SIHANOUK, RUNS TO COMMUNIST CHINA AND NORTH KOREA FOR PROTECTION.
1971-1977 A.D.	FOUR MORE PREACHER TRAINING SCHOOLS ARE HELD AT ADDIS ABABA TRAINING 150 PREACHERS.
1971 A.D.	NIXON ABANDONS THE GOLD STANDARD, DIRECTLY PEGGING MAJOR CURRENCIES TO THE US DOLLAR.
1972 A.D.	STEPHEN JAY GOULD AND NILES ELDRIDGE DEVELOP A THEORY CALLED "PUNCTUATED EQUILIBRIUM" TO HELP JUSTIFY THE FOSSIL RECORD'S FAILURE TO SUPPORT THE THEORY OF EVOLUTION. THEY STRUGGLE TO KEEP EVOLUTION BELIEVABLE.
1973-1977 A.D.	NIXON RESIGNS AS PRESIDENT AND GERALD FORD LEADS THE UNITED STATES.
1973 A.D.	FOLLOWING THE SECOND MAJOR DEVALUATION OF THE US DOLLAR, THE FIXED-RATE CURRENCY EVALUATION MECHANISM IS DISCARDED TO BE REPLACED BY A FLOATING RATE SUBJECT TO THE FORCES OF SUPPLY AND DEMAND.
1973 A.D.	ISRAEL DEFEATS SYRIA AT THE RAMAT DAVID AIRPORT.
1974-1977 A.D.	NORTH VIETNAM LAUNCHES A MAJOR OFFENSIVE. SOUTH VIETNAM FORCES DROP BACK TO SAIGON, LEAVING A

LARGE AMOUNT OF WAR SUPPLIES
BEHIND. SOUTH VIETNAM ASKS TO BE
RE-SUPPLIED, BUT THE U.S. REFUSES.
SOUTH VIETNAM, LAOS, AND CAMBODIA
FALL INTO COMMUNIST HANDS.
NORTH VIETNAM, RUSSIAN TRAINED
AND BACKED FORCES TAKE LAOS AND
SOUTH VIETNAM. COMMUNIST CHINESE
TRAINED AND BACKED KHMER ROUGH
FORCES TAKE CAMBODIA.
RUSSIAN BACKED COMMUNIST FORCES
SEIZE POWER IN ETHIOPIA AND OTHER
EAST AFRICAN NATIONS. OVER 50,000,000
PEOPLE BECOME COMMUNIST SLAVES
FOR THE FIRST TIME. THE   NORTH
VIETNAMESE EXECUTE HUNDREDS OF
THOUSANDS OF SOUTH VIETNAMESE.
MANY FROM SOUTH VIETNAM AND
LAOS ARE SHIPPED TO SLAVE CAMPS
IN EASTERN EUROPE AS PAYMENT
FOR RUSSIAN HELP DURING THE
VIETNAMESE CONFLICT.

1974-1978 A.D.   THE KHMER ROUGH EXECUTE OR
STARVE TO DEATH TWO TO SIX
MILLION PEOPLE. IT IS A CAPITAL
OFFENSE TO BE CAUGHT WITH FOOD
STORES. IT IS A CAPITAL OFFENSE TO
BE EDUCATED, WEAR GLASSES, OR BE
CAUGHT OVER 10 KM. FROM YOUR
HOME. CHILDREN ARE SEPARATED
FROM THEIR PARENTS AFTER FIVE
YEARS OF AGE. THEY ARE MADE TO
WORK IN LEACH INFESTED MUD
BOGS. PARENTS ARE NOT ALLOWED
EVEN TO SEE THEIR CHILDREN AT
NIGHT OR DOCTOR THEIR FESTERING
SORES. FOUR AND FIVE YEAR OLDS ARE
ALLOWED TO SEE THEIR MOTHERS AT
NIGHT, BUT DURING THE DAY THEY

WORK CLEANING MANURE FROM TICK
INFESTED CATTLE PENS. HUSBANDS
AND WIVES ARE KEPT SEPARATE. THE
KHMER ROUGH STEAL EVERYTHING.
THOSE WHO MISS WORK TOO MUCH
ARE PERIODICALLY EXECUTED.
CAMBODIA IS A LARGE SLAVE CAMP.
THOSE THE KHMER ROUGH BECOME
ANGRY WITH ARE CHAINED TO TREES
AND SLOWLY STARVED TO DEATH.
THE COMMUNITY IS PERIODICALLY
MARCHED BY AS THEY STARVE AS AN
OBJECT LESSON.
SOME OF THE SOLDIERS ARE RUTHLESS
FORCING MOTHERS TO KILL THEIR
OWN BABIES AND LAUGHING ABOUT IT.
ETHIOPIA IS NO BETTER. ONE THIRTEEN
YEAR OLD GIRL IS ARRESTED AND
BEATEN EVERY DAY FOR THIRTY DAYS
BECAUSE SHE WILL NOT DENY HER
FAITH IN JESUS.
TEENAGERS THAT SEEM RECEPTIVE
TO INDOCTRINATION ARE SHIPPED
AWAY FOR SIX MONTHS OF INTENSE
INDOCTRINATION. WHEN THEY RETURN
THEY ARE GIVEN GUNS AND TOLD TO
SHOOT WHOEVER IS NOT ACCEPTING
THE INDOCTRINATION. THE RELIGIOUS
GROUPS ARE PLAYED AGAINST ONE
ANOTHER. AT TIMES THE COPTIC STATE
CHURCH IS OUTLAWED. AT OTHER TIME
ALL OTHER CHURCHES ARE OUTLAWED.
DEMERA, A LAWYER AND GOOD
CHRISTIAN BROTHER, IS SELECTED TO
BE THE LEGAL REPRESENTATIVE FOR
THE ADDIS ABABA COMMUNIST URBAN
LEAGUE, THE LARGEST COMMUNIST
ORGANIZATION IN ETHIOPIA. THE
CHURCH OF CHRIST GROWS TO BE

OVER 300 CONGREGATIONS WITH
OVER 50,000 IN ATTENDANCE. OF
THE SOLDIERS BEING USED TO KEEP
ETHIOPIA COMMUNIST, THE CUBANS
ARE THE MOST PITIABLE. THE RUSSIAN
DISRESPECT THEM. THE ETHIOPIANS
DISRESPECT THEM. THEY SEEM TO STAY
DRUNK ALL THE TIME. THEY HAVE NO
FUTURE. IN BATTLE THEY ARE PUT IN
FRONT OF THE RUSSIANS AND IF THEY
BACK UP THE RUSSIANS SHOOT THEM.
THE ETHIOPIANS ARE USED SIMILARLY
IN FRONT OF THE CUBANS, BUT THE
ETHIOPIANS THEY ARE FIGHTING WILL
OFTEN LET THEM GO BY AND SHOOT
THE CUBANS AND RUSSIANS. AFTER THE
FIGHTING IS OVER THE ETHIOPIANS
ARE ACCEPTED BY THE POPULACE.
AS THE RUSSIAN BACKED COMMUNIST
FORCES SEIZE POWER IN ETHIOPIA,
HUNDREDS OF THOUSANDS ARE
EXECUTED. EMPEROR HAILE SELASSIE IS
ASSASSINATED. DURING THE FIRST YEAR
IT IS ESTIMATED THAT OVER 200,000
ARE EXECUTED BY FIRING SQUAD IN
THE FIELD ACROSS FROM THE DEAF
SCHOOL IN ADDIS ABABA. THE CHURCH
CONTINUES TO OPERATE THE DEAF
SCHOOLS. THE COMMUNIST TRY TO
ORGANIZE THE WORKERS TO CREATE
PROBLEMS, BUT THE CHRISTIAN
WORKERS REFUSE TO COMPLAIN
AGAINST THE SCHOOL.
THE GOVERNMENT REQUIRES FATHERS
TO MAKE ONE PROPAGANDA MEETING
EACH SUNDAY AND MOTHERS AND
CHILDREN MAKE OTHERS. THE GOAL
IS TO INDOCTRINATE IN COMMUNISM
AND BREAK DOWN FAMILY LOYALTY.

WIVES AND CHILDREN ARE
ENCOURAGED TO INFORM ON FATHERS
AND HUSBANDS. THE GOVERNMENT
NATIONALIZES NINE TENTHS OF
THE FARM LAND. A FARMER IS TO
CONTINUE TO FARM ALL HIS LAND,
BUT COME HARVEST TIME HE GETS
TO HARVEST ONLY ONE TENTH OF
HIS LAND. THE GOVERNMENT GETS
TO HARVEST THE REST. THEY TRY TO
FORCE THE CHRISTIAN SCHOOLS TO
HIRE COMMUNIST INDOCTRINATORS.
THEY TRY TO FORCE THE CHURCH TO
LET THEM HAVE SIGNATURE RIGHTS
IN THE CHURCH BANK ACCOUNT. IT
BECOMES A CAPITAL OFFENSE TO HAVE
MORE THAN A WEEKS WORTH OF FOOD.
IF YOU DO NOT MAKE THE SUNDAY
PROPAGANDA   MEETINGS YOU DO NOT
RECEIVE PERMISSION TO BUY YOUR
NEXT WEEKS FOOD SUPPLY.

1976-1978 A.D.   THE U.N.'S WORLD HEALTH
ORGANIZATION, IN THEIR
PUBLICATION, FIRST SAY THEY
CAN MAKE A VIRUS THAT FITS THE
DESCRIPTION OF THE AIDS VIRUS. THEY
THEN SUGGEST THAT THEY DO IT.

1977-1981A.D.   JIMMY CARTER IS PRESIDENT OF
THE UNITED STATES. HE CONSIDERS
HIMSELF A "BORN AGAIN CHRISTIAN."
IN EXPLAINING THAT TERM HE SAYS,
"WE BELIEVE THAT THE FIRST TIME
WE'RE BORN, AS CHILDREN IT'S HUMAN
LIFE GIVEN TO US, AND WHEN WE
ACCEPT JESUS AS OUR SAVIOR, IT'S
NEW LIFE...." (QUOTE GIVEN IN 1976).
THE COMMUNIST CHINESE ESPIONAGE
EFFORT OBTAINS INFORMATION
ABOUT THE W-70 NUCLEAR WAR HEAD

(FOR LANCE SHORT RANGE MISSILE
WITH POSSIBLE NEUTRON BOMB
ADAPTATION).
THIS TECHNOLOGICAL BREACH
ALONG WITH THE ONE DURING
THE REAGAN ADMINISTRATION (SEE
1981 A.D.) IS USED BY THE CLINTON
ADMINISTRATION TO TRIVIALIZE THEIR
MASSIVE BREACHES. THE CARTER
ADMINISTRATION NEGOTIATES A
TREATY WITH PANAMA THAT REQUIRES
THE U.S. TO TURN THE PANAMA CANAL
OVER T0 PANAMA BY 2000 A.D. THE US
REMAINS A MILITARY PROTECTORATE
WITH THE RIGHT TO MILITARILY
INTERVENE IF CANAL ACCESS BECOMES
A PROBLEM. AN IN-LAW OF THE
KING OF CAMBODIA, NAREN LOR,
RUNS AWAY AND BECOMES A REFUGEE
IN STOCKTON, CA. MARVIN BLAIR
BAPTIZES HER INTO CHRIST.

1978-1981 A-D THERE IS A BREAK IN THE KHMER
ROUGH LEADERSHIP. POL POT HAS
MISMANAGED THE RICE CROP AND
ORDERS MILLIONS (ABOUT 1/3RD OF THE
COUNTRY) KILLED. HUN SEN BALKS
AT THIS ORDER AND POL POT ORDERS
HUN SEN KILLED. HUN SEN RUNS
TO VIETNAM, AND RETURNS WITH A
VIETNAMESE ARMY. HE HAS PROMISED
THEM CAMBODIAN LAND FOR THEIR
SERVICE. THREE KHMER ROUGH
GENERALS (LATER REFERRED TO AS THE
CAMBODIAN TRIAD) JOIN WITH HUN
SEN. THE FIGHTING CAUSES THE KHMER
ROUGH TO LOOSE CONTROL OF THE
COUNTRYSIDE. MANY CAMBODIANS
SEIZE THE OPPORTUNITY TO RUN.

	SILVER SOARS TO $54/OZ. THE NEW YORK INTERESTS CHANGE THE COMEX TRADING RULES, PERMITTING ONLY SELLING OF SILVER TO THEM, NOT BUYING, PROVING A WILLINGNESS TO "CHEAT" IF THEY AREN'T WINNING. THE HUNT BROTHERS BECOME ONE OF THE BIGGEST BANKRUPTCIES IN U.S. HISTORY.
1979 A.D.	THE SIXTY-NINTH YEAR OF JUBILEE.
1980-1988 A.D.	RONALD WILSON REAGAN IS THE FORTIETH PRESIDENT OF THE UNITED STATES. HE DECLARES, "THE TIME HAS COME TO TURN TO GOD AND REASSERT OUR TRUST IN HIM FOR THE HEALING OF AMERICA...OUR COUNTRY IS IN NEED OF ...A SPIRITUAL RENEWAL..."
1980-1991 A.D.	IRAN AND IRAQ BEGIN A LONG "OFF AND ON "CONFLICT. RUSSIA AND THE U.S. SUPPLY ARMS TO IRAQ AND RUSSIA SUPPLIES ARMS TO IRAN. RUSSIA TRAINS THE OFFICER CORPS OF BOTH ARMIES.
1981A.D.	ETHIOPIAN CHRISTIANS FEEL SEVERELY PERSECUTED. ZENI TEMIE, A YOUNG TEENAGER, IS SMUGGLED OUT BY HER FAMILY (HER FATHER IS A DOCTOR). THEY FEAR THEY WILL NEVER SEE HER AGAIN, BUT WANT HER TO HAVE A FUTURE. CONGRESSMAN SHUMWAY HELPS HER BECOME A LEGAL IMMIGRANT. I AM HER SCIENCE TEACHER AND SHE IS ONE OF THE BRIGHTEST STUDENTS I HAVE EVER TAUGHT. SHE BECOMES PART OF THE STORMY WARD FAMILY.
981-1989A.D.	RONALD REAGAN IS PRESIDENT OF THE UNITED STATES. HE BUILDS UP THE MILITARY AND REDUCES TAXES. THE CHINESE ESPIONAGE EFFORT

OBTAINS INFORMATION ON THE W-88
WAR HEAD (FOR THE TRIDENT II D-5
SUB-LAUNCHED ICBM-8 PER MISSILE).
THIS TECHNOLOGICAL BREACH
(SEE 1977A.D.), IS LATER USED BY
THE CLINTON ADMINISTRATION TO
TRIVIALIZE THEIR MASSIVE BREACHES
(SEE 1997).

1982-1984 A.D.   THE U.N. HIRES INVESTIGATORS TO
DETERMINE IF THEY HAD INTRODUCED
THE AIDS VIRUS AND HAD HELPED
SPREAD IT THROUGH THE WORLD
POPULATIONS. THE INVESTIGATION
ANSWERS, "YES." ANDROPOV LEADS
THE SOVIET UNION.

1984 A.D.   RONALD REAGAN, THE FORTIETH
PRESIDENT OF THE UNITED STATES,
INFORMS HIS AUDIENCE, "WITHOUT
GOD THERE IS NO VIRTUE BECAUSE
THERE IS NO PROMPTING OF THE
CONSCIENCE... WITHOUT GOD THERE
IS A COARSENING OF THE SOCIETY;
WITHOUT GOD DEMOCRACY WILL
NOT AND CANNOT LONG ENDURE... IF
WE EVER FORGET THAT WE ARE ONE
NATION UNDER GOD, THEN WE WILL BE
A NATION GONE UNDER."

1984-1985A.D.   CHERNENKO LEADS THE SOVIET UNION.
THE COMMUNIST REGIME IN ETHIOPIA
MAKES LARGE FOOD SHIPMENTS TO
RUSSIA AND A DEVASTATING FAMINE
BEGINS IN ETHIOPIA. SEVERAL MILLION
PEOPLE DIE FROM THE FAMINE. THE
AMERICAN CHURCHES OF CHRIST
SUPPORT A FEEDING CAMP THAT
FEEDS 35,000 A DAY. THEY ARE NOT
ALLOWED TO FEED IN THE AREA
WHERE THEIR CONGREGATIONS ARE
STRONG (THE MISSION EFFORT HAS

RESULTED IN OVER 50,000 MEMBERS IN
THE SOUTHERN PART OF ETHIOPIA.)
THIS RELIEF EFFORT RESULTS IN
THE CHURCH BEING PLANTED IN
THE NORTHERN, MOSLEM PART OF
ETHIOPIA. AT THE END OF THE FAMINE
THE COMMUNIST ROUND UP BY
FORCE MOST HEALTHY YOUNG PEOPLE
BETWEEN 13 AND 23. THEY ARE SHIPPED
TO SERVE THE COMMUNIST CAUSE IN
ACCORDANCE WITH AN AGREEMENT
BETWEEN THE RULING REGIME AND
RUSSIA. A COLONEL IN THE ETHIOPIAN
ARMY AT THE TIME INFORMS US THAT
THE FIRST GROUP SHIPPED IS TWO
HUNDRED THOUSAND TO ROMANIA
AND THREE HUNDRED THOUSAND TO
CUBA. IT IS KNOWN THAT THERE ARE
FURTHER SLAVE SHIPMENTS. NUMBERS
AND DESTINATIONS ARE NOT KNOWN
TO ME. NONE OF THESE CHILDREN ARE
EVER EXPECTED TO BE PERMITTED TO
HAVE CONTACT WITH THEIR FAMILIES
AGAIN.

1985-1993 A.D.	GORBACHEV LEADS THE SOVIET UNION.
1986 A.D.	THERE IS A NUCLEAR DISASTER AT

CHERNOBYL IN THE UKRAINE, NEAR
ROMANIA. SOME FILMS SUGGEST THAT
PERHAPS ETHIOPIAN YOUTH WERE
USED TO HELP IN THE CLEAN UP.
MANY DIE UNOFFICIALLY. THE AREA
IS EVACUATED. MUCH FARM LAND IS
CONTAMINATED.
THE U.S. LAUNCHES AN AIR ATTACK
AGAINST LIBYA'S MUAMMER GADDAFI.
HE HAD BEEN COOPERATING WITH
TERRORISTS. LIBYA IS BEING LED
TO HATE AMERICA AND LEAN ON THE
SOVIET UNION.

1988-1992 A.D.	GEORGE BUSH SR. IS PRESIDENT OF THE UNITED STATES. HE NEGOTIATES A DISARMAMENT TREATY WITH THE SOVIET UNION.
1989-1997 A.D.	HASHEMI RAFSANJANI RULES IRAN. YATOLLAH ALI HOSEINE KHAMENEI IS CONSIDERED THE ULTIMATE RULER OF IRAN.
1991 A.D.	THE HARD CORE COMMUNIST GOVERNMENT IN ETHIOPIA COLLAPSES AND IS REPLACED BY A SOCIALIST GOVERNMENT. TOP LEADERS ARE STILL NOT ELECTED AND ENEMIES OF THE LEADERS ARE STILL KILLED, BUT NOT OPENLY. THERE IS AN OPEN MARKET AND TRAVEL ABOUT THE COUNTRY IS EASY. IRAQ SEIZES KUWAIT. THE U.S. ORGANIZES A LIBERATION FORCE AND DRIVES IRAQ OUT. THE BEST OF IRAQI AIR POWER IS FLOWN TO IRAN TO ESCAPE DESTRUCTION.
1991-1997 A.D.	CAMBODIA HAS U.N. SUPERVISED ELECTIONS AND KING SIHANOUK'S PARTY WINS. HE RETURNS FROM COMMUNIST CHINA WITH NORTH KOREAN BODY GUARDS. ALTHOUGH HUN SEN LOST THE ELECTION, HE IS PERMITTED TO CO-RULE TO AVOID WAR.

CHAPTER THIRTEEN
A CHRISTIAN CHRONOLOGY OF HISTORY
(1992 A.D. – 2008 A.D.)
A TIME LINE OF HUMAN HISTORY
FROM A CHRISTIAN PROSPECTIVE
Compiled by "God's Friend"

1992 A.D.

TED TURNER AND NEW WIFE JANE FONDA SUPPORT THE ELECTION OF BILL CLINTON, A FORMER NORTH VIETNAMESE SYMPATHIZER WHO RECEIVED SOME TRAINING IN RUSSIA. BY NOW TED TURNER'S NEWS CASTING HOLDINGS ARE SOME OF THE MOST POWERFUL IN THE UNITED STATES (SEE 1967 AND 1980 A.D.). BILL CLINTON REPORTEDLY HAS TIES TO MAJOR COCAINE DEALERS AND CLOSE ASSOCIATES SAY HE IS PROTECTING THEM AND LAUNDERING THEIR MONEY THROUGH ARKANSAS STATE AGENCIES. CLINTON HAS PARDONED HIS FRIEND, DAN LASATER, AFTER HE WAS CONVICTED AS A MAJOR DRUG TRAFFICKER. REPORTS SAY THEY ARE LAUNDERING $100,000,000.00 PER MONTH. THE MONEY GOES TO MAKE LOANS TO CLINTON SUPPORTERS THAT THEY DO NOT HAVE TO REPAY. THE DRUG TRAFFICKERS (LASATER ET AL) GET ARKANSAS BONDS FOR THEIR CASH WITH BOND SALES COMMISSIONS AND ACCUMULATING INTEREST. THE ONLY

LOSERS ARE ARKANSAS TAX PAYERS WHEN THE BONDS COME DUE. (SEE DVD: "THE CLINTON CHRONICLES")

1992 A.D. GEORGE BUSH, THE FORTY FIRST PRESIDENT OF THE UNITED STATES, PRAYS, "THE LORD OUR GOD BE WITH US AS HE WAS WITH OUR FATHERS; MAY HE NOT LEAVE US OR FORSAKE US; SO THAT HE MAY INCLINE OUR HEARTS TO HIM TO WALK IN ALL HIS WAYS... THAT ALL THE PEOPLE OF THE EARTH MAY KNOW THAT THE LORD IS GOD; THERE IS NO OTHER."

1993 A.D. THE SOVIET UNION DISSOLVES AND DOES NOT FULFILL ITS OBLIGATIONS UNDER THE DISARMAMENT TREATY. CLINTON LEADS THE UNITED STATES TO CONTINUE UNILATERAL DISARMAMENT UNDER THE TREATY. YELTSIN BECOMES THE LEADER OF THE COMMUNIST NATIONS THAT WERE KNOWN AS THE SOVIET UNION. HE IS PRESIDENT OF RUSSIA. CLINTON APPOINTS A RELATIVE, JANET RENO, AS U.S. ATTORNEY GENERAL. SHE FIRES ALL 93 U.S. ATTORNEYS AND STOPS THE INVESTIGATIONS INTO CLINTON'S WHITEWATER SCANDAL. KATHLEEN WILLEY IS SEXUALLY ASSAULTED BY CLINTON IN HIS OFFICE AND CONFIDES IN LINDA TRIPP, A SECRETARY IN THE WHITE HOUSE COUNSEL'S OFFICE. LINDA TRIPP SOMETIMES WORKS WITH VINCENT FOSTER JR. VINCENT FOSTER JR., A LAWYER WORKING FOR CLINTON, IS PROBABLY MURDERED AND THEN DROPPED IN A PARK NEAR THE WHITE HOUSE. CLINTON DECLARES H DEATH A "SUICIDE." ONE OF VINCEN

BODY GUARDS ENDS UP DEAD A FEW
DAYS LATER. CLINTON, FOR THE FIRST
TIME IN HISTORY, BEGINS REQUIRING
AMERICAN SOLDIERS, WHO PLEDGED
THEIR ALLEGIANCE TO THE UNITED
STATES, TO ACCEPT COMMANDERS
FROM FOREIGN NATIONS WHO DO NOT
HAVE THAT ALLEGIANCE, OR BE COURT
MARSHALED OUT OF THE MILITARY.
THIS IS ILLEGAL, BUT HE DOES IT
ANYWAY. ONE OF THE FIRST TOP
COMMANDERS THEY ARE REQUIRED
TO OBEY IN BOSNIA IS A PERSON WITH
ALLEGIANCE TO IRAQ AND SADDAM
HUSSEIN.

1994-1998 A.D.   LINDA TRIPP IS SUBPOENAED TO
TESTIFY ABOUT THE KATHLEEN WILLEY
INCIDENT IN THE PAULA JONES CASE.
AFTER HER TESTIMONY THE WHITE
HOUSE USES ITS POWER TO SMEAR
HER CHARACTER, AND TRANSFERS HER
TO THE PUBLIC AFFAIRS OFFICE AT
THE PENTAGON. CLINTON THEN HAS
AN AFFAIR WITH MONICA LEWINSKY.
WHEN HE DECIDES TO COOL THE
AFFAIR DOWN HE TRANSFERS MONICA
TO THE PENTAGON PUBLIC AFFAIRS
OFFICE WHERE MONICA CONFIDES IN
LINDA. THE AFFAIR IS DOCUMENTED IN
TESTIMONY.
CLINTON LIES ABOUT IT UNDER OATH,
ATTEMPTING TO OBSTRUCT JUSTICE
THROUGH A NUMBER OF MEANS.
HE ENDS UP BEING IMPEACHED,
BUT THE SENATE, EXCEPT FOR TWO
BRAVE DEMOCRATS, VOTES DOWN
PARTY LINES. DURING THE HOUSE
IMPEACHMENT PROCEEDINGS CLINTON
APPEARS TO USE THE ILLEGALLY

HELD FBI FILES (SEE 1996) TO TRY TO
EMBARRASS REPUBLICAN LEADERS.
TWO MAJORITY LEADERS RESIGN.
AFTER THE IMPEACHMENT CLINTON
DECLARES A VENDETTA AGAINST
THE HOUSE MANAGERS WHO DID
THEIR DUTY AND BROUGHT THE
IMPEACHMENT CASE.

1995 A.D.   MANY VILLAGES IN CENTRAL AFRICA
BECOME UNINHABITED DUE TO AIDS.
THE CLINTON ADMINISTRATION
APPEARS TO BEGIN MANIPULATING
THE GOLD MARKET. THIS MAKES THE
DOLLAR SEEM MUCH STRONGER THAN
IT MERITS AND INTERFERES WITH
NORMAL INTEREST RATE ADJUSTMENTS.

1996 A.D.   COMMUNIST CHINA APPEARS TO
ILLEGALLY FUNNEL MILLIONS OF
DOLLARS INTO CLINTON'S REELECTION
FUNDS. THEY ALSO REPORTEDLY PUT A
MILLION DOLLARS INTO HIS PERSONAL
LEGAL DEFENSE FUND. THEY APPEAR
ALSO TO CONTRIBUTE HEAVILY TO AN
APPARENT $1,000,000.00 BRIBE GIVEN
WEBSTER HUBBELL FOR SILENCE.
THEN COMMUNIST CHINA RECEIVES
BASES OF OPERATIONS ON BOTH
ENDS OF THE PANAMA CANAL AND IN
LONG BEACH, CA. CONGRESS PASSES
A LAW BLOCKING THEIR CONTINUED
USE OF THE LONG BEACH PORT OF
ENTRY AFTER THEY ARE CAUGHT
BRING IN THOUSANDS OF AUTOMATIC
WEAPONS. OVER A HUNDRED
THOUSAND MEXICAN FELONS ARE
ILLEGALLY NATIONALIZED TO VOTE
IN THE CALIFORNIA SYSTEM AND THE
RIGHT OF AMERICANS TO CHOOSE
THEIR OWN LEADERS IS TAMPERED

WITH. THE BRITISH TURN HONG KONG OVER TO COMMUNIST CHINA DESPITE THE CITIZENS' OBJECTIONS. CHINA DISSOLVES HONG KONG'S ELECTED LEGISLATURE AND APPOINTS THEIR OWN. BY THIS TIME ABOUT 50 ASSOCIATES OF BILL CLINTON HAVE HAD QUESTIONABLE "SUICIDES" OR FATAL "ACCIDENTS" JUST BEFORE THEY ARE TO BECOME AN EMBARRASSMENT FOR BILL CLINTON. RON BROWN IS IN THE CHAIN OF COMMAND OF A COMMUNIST CHINESE AGENT WHO HAS BEEN GIVEN TOP SECRET CLEARANCE AT BILL CLINTON'S ORDER (THE FBI NEVER DID THE BACKGROUND INVESTIGATION REQUIRED FOR CANDIDATES FOR TOP SECRET CLEARANCE). HE HAS HELPED FUNNEL FUNDS FROM RED CHINA INTO ACCOUNTS THAT SUPPORT CLINTON. BROWN IS ALSO A MAIN OPERATIVE TO GIVE TAXPAYER HELP IN SETTING UP FOREIGN BUSINESSES FOR CAMPAIGN CONTRIBUTIONS.
BROWN IS CALLED ON TO TESTIFY IN A CONGRESSIONAL INVESTIGATION. HE AND CLINTON HAVE A FALLING OUT AND HE IS ORDERED TO TAKE A TRIP TO BOSNIA BEFORE HE TESTIFIES. DURING THE TRIP RON BROWN DIES IN AN AIR PLANE CRASH WITH A NUMBER OF AMERICAN BUSINESSMEN. CLINTON DECLARES HIS DEATH AN "ACCIDENT"AND ORDERS NO AUTOPSY. THE MILITARY DOES AN AUTOPSY AND FINDS A 45 SLUG THROUGH THE HEAD AS THE PROBABLE CAUSE FOR BROWN'S DEATH. A NUMBER OF MILITARY PERSONNEL KILLED IN THE "ACCIDENT"

HAVE DRAWN WEAPONS AS THOUGH
THEY ARE TRYING TO DEFEND BROWN.
CHARLES MEISSNER, THE IMMEDIATE
SUPERVISOR OF JOHN HUANG, THE
COMMUNIST CHINA AGENT, IS ALSO
KILLED IN THE PLANE CRASH. ONE OF
THE MILITARY ATTENDANTS SURVIVES
THE CRASH AND WALKS AROUND FOR
OVER AN HOUR BEFORE RESCUE UNITS
ARRIVE. AS THE UNITS BEGIN TO OFFER
HER AID A HELICOPTER OF SPECIAL
FORCE TROOPS ARRIVE AND INSIST
SHE GOES TO THE HOSPITAL WITH
THEM. SHE DIES OF A BROKEN NECK
BEFORE SHE REACHES THE HOSPITAL.
CLINTON CLAIMS STORM CONDITIONS
CONTRIBUTED TO THE CRASH.
MILITARY PERSONNEL CLAIM THERE
WERE NO STORM CONDITIONS.
A GUIDANCE BEACON IS MISSING
AND THE GROUND CREW SARGENT
REVEALING THE MISSING GUIDANCE
BEACON AND NO STORM CONDITIONS
ENDS UP DEAD.
THE LEAD MILITARY INCIDENT
INVESTIGATOR QUESTIONS CLINTON'S
CLAIM IT IS AN "ACCIDENT". CLINTON
SENDS AN ENVOY TO TALK TO THE TOP
MILITARY OFFICER RESPONSIBLE FOR
THE PLANE CRASH INVESTIGATION.
AFTER THE ENVOY LEAVES THE OFFICER
IS FOUND WITH A 45 SLUG THROUGH
HIS HEART. CLINTON DECLARES THIS
DEATH A "SUICIDE" AND DEMOTES AND
DRIVES THE AUTOPSY PARTICIPATING
PERSONNEL FROM THE MILITARY.
CLINTON STILL PUBLICLY MAINTAINS
THAT BROWN'S DEATH IS ACCIDENT
ABOUT A MONTH AFTERWARDS

BROWN'S SECRETARY IS FOUND IN HER
WASHINGTON, D.C. OFFICE NAKED
AND DEAD. THIS SCANDAL BECOMES
KNOWN AS "CHINAGATE." IN THIS
SAME YEAR IT IS LEARNED THAT THE
WHITE HOUSE ILLEGALLY HAS IN
ITS POSSESSION FBI BACK GROUND
FILES ON MORE THAN 900 LEADING
REPUBLICANS. THESE FILES CONTAIN
RAW, UNVERIFIED INFORMATION
TO INCLUDE RUMORS AND GOSSIP.
THE SUDANESE GOVERNMENT HAS
A FALLING OUT WITH OSAMA BIN
LADEN AND HAS HIM MOVE HIS MAIN
TERRORIST BASE FROM THEIR COUNTRY
TO AFGHANISTAN. CLINTON TURNS
DOWN AN OPPORTUNITY TO ARREST
HIM.

1997 A.D.   RUSSIA WORKS ON BUILDING A
NUCLEAR POWER PLANT IN IRAN
GIVING THEM POTENTIAL NUCLEAR
WEAPONS CAPABILITIES. SEYED
MOHAMMAD KHATAMI BECOMES
THE PRESIDENT (RULER) OF IRAN.
AYATOLLAH ALI HOSEINE KHAMENEI
CONTINUES TO BE THE ULTIMATE
RULER OF IRAN.
HUN SEN LEADS A COUP IN CAMBODIA.
HE PROCLAIMS THAT HE IS GOING TO
BUILD CAMBODIAN SCHOOLS WITH
DRUG MONEY. DURING THE COUP,
OFFICIALS WHO INTERFERED WITH
DRUG TRAFFIC ARE TORTURED AND
KILLED. HUN SEN DOES NOT SEEM TO
HAVE THIS DRUG STANCE IN FUTURE
YEARS.

97-1999 A.D.   U.S. ATTORNEY GENERAL RENO
BLOCKS INVESTIGATIONS INTO
CHINAGATE (A CHINESE ESPIONAGE

SCANDAL INVOLVING CLINTON, CAMPAIGN CONTRIBUTIONS, AND THE COMMERCE DEPARTMENT) BY KEN STARR. JUDICIAL WATCH, A PRIVATE FUNDED ORGANIZATION SUPPORTED BY VOLUNTARY CONTRIBUTIONS, BECOMES THE NATION'S BEST PROTECTION. THE HEAD OF THE F.B.I. AND HER OWN HEAD OF INVESTIGATIONS NOTIFY RENO IN WRITING OF HER OBLIGATION, UNDER LAW, TO TURN THE SCANDAL OVER TO AN INDEPENDENT COUNSEL. SHE REFUSES. JUDICIAL WATCH'S INVESTIGATION RESULTS IN OVER FIFTY PERSONS CLOSELY ASSOCIATED WITH THE CLINTON ADMINISTRATION AND INVOLVED IN CHINAGATE EITHER PLEADING THE 5TH AMENDMENT OR SEEKING POLITICAL ASYLUM IN COMMUNIST CHINA. COMMUNIST CHINA BEGINS A MASSIVE MILITARY BUILD UP CONTRIBUTING TO AN ASIAN ECONOMIC CRASH (THE HONG KONG STOCK MARKET LOOSES OVER HALF ITS VALUE). ATTORNEY GENERAL RENO BEGINS BLOCKING F.B.I. EFFORTS TO INVESTIGATE CHINESE ESPIONAGE AT THE DEPARTMENT OF ENERGY (THIS APPEARS TO PERMIT THE MAJOR SUSPECT TO CONTINUE TO SUPPLY INFORMATION TO COMMUNIST CHINA FOR THREE EXTRA YEARS). THE COMMUNIST CHINESE STEAL LEGACY CODES (COMPUTER CODES WITH 50 YEARS OF U.S. NUCLEAR TESTING KNOWLEDGE AND DESIGN INFORMATION), WARHEAD SIMULATION TECHNOLOGY

(ENABLES ONE TO DEVELOP AND
MAINTAIN NUCLEAR WEAPONS
WITHOUT   ACTUAL TESTING),
ELECTROMAGNETIC TECHNOLOGY
(USEFUL IN SPACE-BASED ANTI-
SATELLITE AND ANTIMISSILE
SYSTEMS), ANTISUBMARINE
TECHNOLOGY (SPACE-BASED RADAR
TO DETECT SUBMERGED SUBMARINES),
MISSILE NOSE CONE TECHNOLOGY
(IMPROVES THE RELIABILITY OF
BALLISTIC MISSILES), AND OVER
200 PAGES OF OTHER COX REPORT
NUCLEAR INFORMATION THE CLINTON
ADMINISTRATION SAYS CANNOT BE
MADE PUBLIC. IT APPEARS THAT THE
CHINESE ALSO OBTAIN PLANS FOR THE
FOLLOWING U.S. WAR   HEADS: W-87
WARHEAD (FOR PEACE KEEPER SILO-
BASED ICBM-10 PER MISSILE), W-78
WARHEAD (FOR MINUTEMAN MARK
12A SILO-BASED ICBM-3 PER MISSILE),
W-76 WARHEAD (FOR TRIDENT IC-4 SUB
LAUNCHED ICBM-8 PER MISSILE), W-62
WARHEAD (MINUTEMAN III SILO-BASED
ICBM-3 PER MISSILE), W-56 WARHEAD
(FOR MINUTEMAN II SILO-BASED
ICBM-1 PER MISSILE), THE NEUTRON
BOMB (NEVER DEPLOYED ENHANCED
RADIATION WEAPON-KILLS PEOPLE,
BUT LEAVES STRUCTURES STANDING),
AND REENTRY VEHICLES (HEAT SHIELD
PROTECTING WARHEADS AS THEY
REENTER EARTH'S ATMOSPHERE).
CLINTON ALSO ORDERED MASSIVE
AMOUNTS OF NUCLEAR INFORMATION
DECLASSIFIED, AND STOPPED FBI
BACKGROUND CHECKS FOR WORKERS
AND VISITORS AT THE WEAPONS LABS.

HE LEAKED CLASSIFIED INFORMATION
TO THE MEDIA, SWITCHED EXPORT
LICENSE AUTHORITY FOR SATELLITES
AND MILITARY-RELATED TECHNOLOGY
TO AN AGENCY COMMERCE MINDED
AND NOT MILITARY SECURITY MINDED.
HE GRANTED WAIVERS, ALLOWING
MISSILE TECHNOLOGY TRANSFERS
TO COMMUNIST CHINA, RELAXED
SECURITY-BASED TRADE RESTRICTIONS,
AND PERMITTED STATE OF THE
ART COMPUTER SALES THAT WERE
DIVERTED TO COMMUNIST CHINA'S
MILITARY BUILDUP. CLINTON
USES TECHNOLOGICAL BREACHES
DURING THE CARTER AND REAGAN
ADMINISTRATIONS TO TRIVIALIZE
THE BREACHES DURING HIS
ADMINISTRATION (SEE 1977 AND
1981 A.D.). TOP MILITARY CHINESE
GENERALS BEGIN BOASTING THAT THE
Y2K PROBLEM WILL ELIMINATE THE
U.S. TECHNOLOGICAL ADVANTAGE.
THEY ALSO SAY THE U.S. IS THE MAIN
OBSTACLE TO THE ACCOMPLISHMENT
OF COMMUNIST CHINA'S EXPANSION
GOALS. THE CLINTON ADMINISTRATION
BEGINS TO USE VOCABULARY THAT
INDICATES THEIR WILLINGNESS TO
LET COMMUNIST CHINA SEIZE TAIWAN.
THERE IS A TREATY THAT WOULD
REQUIRE THE U.S. TO WITHDRAW FROM
PANAMA BY THE END OF 1999 WHILE
STILL GUARANTEEING ACCESS. PANAMA
TRIES TO NEGOTIATE A TREATY THAT
WOULD GUARANTEE THAT U.S. TROOPS
WOULD STAY THERE BEYOND 1999 (SEE
1976 AND 1996 A.D.). THE CLINTON
ADMINISTRATION SABOTAGES THIS

EFFORT. BY THE END OF THIS PERIOD
OVER 70 ASSOCIATES WHO HAVE
BECOME A POLITICAL EMBARRASSMENT
FOR BILL CLINTON HAVE OFFICIALLY
COMMITTED "SUICIDE" OR HAD A
FATAL "ACCIDENT."
NOT ONLY CAN YOU FOLLOW THE
CLINTON ADMINISTRATION'S SCANDALS
BY FOLLOWING THE MONEY, BUT THE
MORE OBVIOUS TRAIL IS THE CORPSE
TRAIL. CLINTON SEEMS TO FOLLOW
STALIN'S USE OF POLITICAL ALLIES.
AT THE BEGINNING OF THIS PERIOD
COMMUNIST CHINA COULD NOT
DELIVER NUCLEAR WAR HEADS FROM
THEIR HOMELAND TO TARGETS IN THE
U.S.
BY THE END OF THIS PERIOD THEY CAN
AND HAVE TARGETED U.S. CITIES WITH
THEIR MISSILES. CHINESE GENERALS
WRITE THAT IN WAR YOU SHOULD
DESTROY YOUR ENEMY'S ECONOMY
PRIOR TO ACTUAL COMBAT, SO THAT HE
CAN NOT FINANCE HIS FIGHT AGAINST
YOU.

1998 A.D.   THE MISSION WORK IN ETHIOPIA
BEGINS TRAINING A HUNDRED NEW
PREACHERS A YEAR. THERE ARE OVER
600 CONGREGATIONS WITH OVER
60,000 CHRISTIANS IN ATTENDANCE.
WAR IS RAGGING ALONG THE
NORTHERN BOARDER OF ETHIOPIA
AND OVER FLOWING INTO SUDAN
AND SOMALIA. CAMBODIA HAS A
GENERAL ELECTION WITH MANY
IRREGULARITIES. THE THREE GROUPS
RUNNING FOR ELECTION ARE PARTIES
HEADED BY KING SIHANOUK, HUN
SEN, AND SAM RAINSY. NO PARTY WINS

A CLEAR MAJORITY. THE SIHANOUK AND HUN SEN PARTIES AGREE TO TRY TO SHARE POWER AGAIN (SEE 1991, 1997 A.D.). THE SAM RAINSY PARTY REFUSES TO SHARE POWER "WITH SUCH ELECTION HYPOCRISY."

1999 A.D. THE CLINTON ADMINISTRATION LEADS NATO TO BOMB KOSOVO AND SERBIA. THIS INFURIATES RUSSIA, CHINA, AND SERBIA. YELTSIN, PRESIDENT OF RUSSIA, BEGINS INTERRUPTING SPEECHES ON UNRELATED SUBJECTS TO RAGE AGAINST CLINTON AND THE U.S. MOST OF THE BOMBING IS CONDUCTED FROM HIGH ELEVATIONS AND IT DAMAGES CIVILIAN TARGETS, KILLING MANY CIVILIANS. THE CHURCH OF CHRIST MEETING PLACE IN BELGRADE IS DESTROYED. THIS GROUP OF CHRISTIANS PLAYED A MAJOR ROLE IN THE BIBLE SMUGGLING OPERATIONS DURING THE COLD WAR BETWEEN RUSSIA AND THE U.S. AN ESTIMATED 11,000 ANTIPERSONNEL EXPLOSIVE DEVICES FROM NATO CLUSTER BOMBS ARE LEFT AS BOOBY TRAPS SCATTERED ACROSS KOSOVO (THE CLUSTER BOMBS HAVE A KNOWN RATE OF FAILURE TO INITIALLY DETONATE AND THIS FIGURE CAN BE OBTAINED BY APPLYING THAT KNOWN RATE TO THE NUMBER OF BOMBS DROPPED). WHEN ONE BLOWS UP, KILLING BRITISH SOLDIERS AND CIVILIANS, CLINTON BLAMES IT ON SERB PLANTED MINES. AFTER NATO FORCES ENTER KOSOVO TO REPLACE THE SERB POLICE FORCES, GERMAN NATO FORCES FIND A MASS GRAVE.

RETURNING ALBANIANS MASSACRE 17 SERB FARMERS, AND THERE IS A LOT OF EVERYBODY BLAMING EVERYBODY ELSE. DRUG TRAFFIC THROUGH KOSOVO EXPLODES. THE ALBANIANS DO NOT DISARM ACCORDING TO THE TREATY. RUSSIA BEGINS REPLACING OLDER MISSILES WITH TOPOL-M MISSILES. SHE BUILDS UP MILITARY SUPPORT UNITS. RUSSIA ALSO BEGINS TO INCREASE MISSILE PRODUCTION PROGRAMS WITH A GENERAL BUILD UP OF NAVAL FORCES. THE RUSSIAN PARLIAMENT FAILS TO RATIFY THE START II TREATY WITH THE U.S. WEEKLY THE U.S. AND BRITAIN ARE ALSO BOMBING IRAQ MISSILE PLACEMENTS.

IRANIAN NEWS AGENCIES CONTINUALLY REFER TO THE "CRIMES" OF BILL CLINTON AND PRIME MINISTER TONY BLAIR AGAINST THE IRAQI PEOPLE. THEY SAY THE AIR RAIDS OVER IRAQ ARE AGAINST INTERNATIONAL LAW, WITHOUT PRIOR U.N. KNOWLEDGE OR SANCTION. THE U.S. PASSES OIL SANCTIONS AGAINST IRAN AND LIBYA (SEE 597 B.C., 57 A.D., AND 96 A.D.). THERE DEVELOPS A MOVE IN THE CAMBODIAN GOVERNMENT TO RETURN CAMBODIA TO A FORM OF COMMUNISM. CAMBODIA FORMS ALLIANCES WITH COMMUNIST CHINA AND VIETNAM. A LARGE NUMBER OF LEGISLATORS RESIGN, AND URGE THE PEOPLE TO SUPPORT THE SAM RAINSY PARTY. THEY THEN RUN OFF TO THAILAND. THE CAMBODIAN GOVERNMENT BEGINS A DRIVE TO DISARM THE CAMBODIAN PEOPLE. AT

THE END OF JULY CLINTON ORDERS ALL
U.S. TROOPS TO LEAVE PANAMA.
THIS WOULD REQUIRE COMMUNIST
CHINESE COOPERATION FOR AMERICAN
SHIPPING TO GO FROM NEW YORK TO
LOS ANGELES, OR THAT SHIPPING TO
EITHER GO ALL THE WAY AROUND THE
WORLD OR BRAVE THE ANTARCTIC SEAS
SOUTH OF SOUTH AMERICA. DAMAGE
TO THE RESERVOIR PROVIDING WATER
TO THE CANAL'S LOCKS COULD DISABLE
THE CANAL FOR TWO TO THREE YEARS
AFTER THE RESERVOIR REPAIR.
U.S. ARMY COLONEL DAVID FRANZ AND
FORMER C.I.A. AGENT LARRY HARRIS
SAY DEBRIEFINGS OF TERRORISTS
INDICATE IRAQ, IRAN, LIBYA, SUDAN
AND OTHER COUNTRIES ARE NOW
OPERATING UNDER THE RELIGIOUS
NOTION THAT THE ADVENT OF THE
YEAR TWO THOUSAND SIGNALS THEIR
LAST CHANCE TO FULFILL THEIR
SACRED MORAL DUTY TO DESTROY
THE UNITED STATES, WHICH THEY
CONSIDER "THE GREAT SATAN." AGENTS
OF THESE COUNTRIES BELIEVE THEY
WILL OBTAIN A SPECIAL PLACE IN
HEAVEN IF THEY ANNIHILATE ENOUGH
AMERICAN CITIZENS. THEY BELIEVE
THEY CAN REDUCE THE AMERICAN
POPULATION BY TWO THIRDS IN
A SHORT PERIOD OF TIME. C.I.A.
INFORMATION INDICATES THERE ARE
OVER 100 TERRORIST "CELL" TEAMS
SECRETED THROUGH OUT MAJOR
U.S. CITIES, EACH IN POSSESSION
OF DOZENS OF VIALS OF DEADLY
ANTHRAX AND BUBONIC PLAGUE
BACTERIA. THEY INTEND TO SPRAY

THESE DEADLY BIOLOGICAL AGENTS
INTO THE AIR WITH SPECIAL SPRAYING
DEVICES CALLED "VENTURIS." THE
CELLS ARE SUPPOSEDLY TARGETING
120 LARGE AMERICAN CITIES DURING
CHRISTMAS RUSH TIME. THEY EXPECT
TO ACCOMPLISH THEIR SLAUGHTER IN
LESS THAN TWO WEEKS. (SEE 597-587
B.C.-EZE. 38, 39, 57-58 A.D., 62-63 A.D.,
96-97 A.D.-REV. 20:7-9). THE CLINTON
ADMINISTRATION KNOWS ABOUT
THIS WELL IN ADVANCE, BUT DOES
NOT DEVELOP ONE PROGRAM FOR
TEACHING AMERICAN CITIZENS HOW
TO SURVIVE.
INSTEAD THEY TRAIN FEDERAL AGENTS
ON HOW TO CLEAN UP THE DEAD AND
DYING, HOW TO SEIZE CONTROL OF
KEY INDUSTRIES AND UTILITIES, HOW
TO ENFORCE CURFEWS AND LIMIT
CIVILIAN TRAVEL. ON SEPT.2 CONGRESS
MAKES IT A FELONY TO EXPORT GAS
MASKS THAT PROTECT AGAINST
BIOLOGICAL WARFARE. BUBONIC
PLAGUE IS NORMALLY TREATABLE WITH
STREPTOMYCIN, BUT NOT PENICILLIN.
THE PREFERRED TREATMENT FOR
ANTHRAX IS PENICILLIN. BOTH ARE
TREATABLE WITH TETRACYCLINE. IT
BECOMES PUBLIC KNOWLEDGE THAT
JOHN HUANG HAS TURNED STATES
EVIDENCE IN CHINAGATE. BEFORE
IT BECOMES KNOWN HE TAPES HIS
CHINA CONTACT TELLING HIM NOT TO
DIVULGE CLINTON OR A HIGH RANKING
COMMUNIST GENERAL'S ROLL IN THE
SCANDAL. THE LIVES OF HIM AND HIS
FAMILY ARE THREATENED IF HE DOES
AND HE IS PROMISED A PRESIDENTIAL

PARDON IF HE DOESN'T. HE ASKS ABOUT THE SURETY OF THE PARDON AND IS TOLD CLINTON KNOWS WHAT IS GOING ON AND WOULDN'T DARE GO BACK ON HIS WORD. AS THIS INFORMATION BECOMES KNOWN, THE WHITEHOUSE REVISITS TULSA AND RENO ATTEMPTS TO DISCREDIT THE F.B.I. IT APPEARS A MOVE IS IN THE MAKING TO REPLACE THE TOP COMMAND POSITIONS OF THE F.B.I.

2000 A.D. THE MUCH FEARED Y2K TECHNOLOGY PROBLEM DOES NOT MATERIALIZE. SUDAN'S GOVERNMENT IS SUPPORTING SLAVE TRADERS WHO RAID CHRISTIAN VILLAGES, PILLAGING, KILLING AND ENSLAVING SURVIVORS. THEIR DECLARED GOAL IS AFRICAN CONQUEST FOLLOWED BY WORLD CONQUEST IN THE NAME OF ALLAH. GEORGE BUSH IS ELECTED PRESIDENT OF THE UNITED STATES. SOME CLAIM THE CLINTON ADMINISTRATION HAS DISPOSED OF OVER 80% OF THE U.S. GOLD RESERVES MANIPULATING A LOW GOLD PRICE AND STRONG DOLLAR. THE NASDAQ ENTERS A VICIOUS BEAR MARKET. J.P. MORGAN AND CHASE, MAJOR U.S. BANKING CONCERNS, HAVE ENDED UP LEVERAGED 650 TIMES THEIR NET WORTH. THEIR POSITIONS ARE SHORT GOLD AND LONG INTEREST RATES MADE PROFITABLE BY A DECLINING PRICE OF GOLD. (THEY PROVIDED CLINTON'S SECRETARY OF TREASURY WHO IS CLAIMED TO HAVE PARTICIPATED IN THE MANIPULATIONS THAT COST THE U.S. MOST OF HER

GOLD RESERVES). THE DEUTSCHE BANK, BUNDES BANK, IMF AND GOLD SWAPS SEEM TO PLAY A ROLE IN THE DISAPPEARANCE OF THE U.S. GOLD RESERVES. THE BUNDESBANK GAINS OWNERSHIP OF ABOUT 1700 TONS OF U.S. GOLD. LATER THE DEUTSCHE BANK HELPS CLINTON OBTAIN REAL ESTATE HE SHOULD NOT QUALIFY TO BUY. CLINTON IS LEAVING THE U.S. BANKING SYSTEM ON THE VERGE OF COLLAPSE. CLINTON SPENDS THE LAST FEW MONTHS OF HIS ADMINISTRATION GETTING ISRAEL AND THE PALESTINIANS TO DISCUSS THE FATE OF JERUSALEM. THIS SUBJECT HAS BEEN A SOURCE OF WAR FOR OVER A 1000 YEARS AND SHOULD BE A SURE WAY TO CAUSE CONFLICT, STIRRING UP MOSLEM HATRED TOWARD THE U.S. AND ISRAEL. BOB BERARD OPENS UP A MISSION IN PHNOM PENH AND, WITH CHOEU LORK, ESTABLISHES THE PHNOM PENH CHURCH OF CHRIST.

2001 A.D. GEORGE BUSH ASSUMES THE DUTIES OF THE PRESIDENT OF THE UNITED STATES. THE DOW FOLLOWS THE NASDAQ INTO A BEAR MARKET. GOLD ENTERS A BULL MARKET. THE CONFLICT IN THE MIDDLE EAST ESCALATES. DURING THE SUMMER MOSES SETH AND BILL SINGLETON TRAVEL THROUGH CAMBODIA VISITING CHURCHES. OVER 100 ARE BAPTIZED INTO CHRIST. AMONG THOSE BAPTIZED ARE ANH PAULEY AND HIS FAMILY. THE CHRISTIAN FAITH IS SPREADING RAPIDLY IN CAMBODIA. THERE IS AN INADEQUATE SUPPLY OF BIBLES AND

GOOD BIBLE TEACHING FOLLOW-UP. KIM VORARITSKUL OF THE KHON KAEN THAILAND BIBLE INSTITUTE OFFERS TO TRAIN 4 OR 5 CAMBODIANS IN THE THAI SCHOOL IF THEY CAN READ AND SPEAK FLUENT THAI. VORARITSKUL IS TRAINING ABOUT 30 PREACHERS EVERY SIX MONTHS FOR THAILAND. LAOS HAS BASICALLY OUTLAWED CHRISTIANITY, ARRESTING WORSHIPERS AND INCARCERATING THEM IN RE-TRAINING INSTITUTIONS UNTIL THEY DENOUNCE THE CHRISTIAN FAITH. THEY ARE BEING GUIDED BY CHINESE ADVISORS. THE KINGS PARTY (CLOSELY ASSOCIATED WITH COMMUNIST CHINA) HAS ESTABLISHED MOSLEM TRAINING CAMPS ACROSS CAMBODIA. WE CONTACT TRUMAN SCOTT AND ASK FOR THE SUNSET INTERNATIONAL BIBLE INSTITUTE TO ESTABLISH A SCHOOL OF PREACHING IN CAMBODIA. HE SEEMS POSITIVE ABOUT IT, AND FOLLOWS UP WITH PLANNING DISCUSSIONS WITH TRUITT ADAIR. SAM RAINSY REPORTS THAT HUN SEN HAS KILLED SEVERAL OF HIS PARTY'S CANDIDATES AND ARRESTED OTHERS. THERE IS AN ELECTION IN CAMBODIA SCHEDULED FOR FEBRUARY OF 2002. WHILE WE WERE IN PHNOM PENH A BOMB DESTROYED A HOTEL THAT PROVIDED INCOME FOR THE KING'S PARTY. INVESTIGATIONS POINTED TO MEMBERS OF HUN SEN'S PARTY. BIN LADIN'S AL-QAIDA TERRORIST MOSLEM GROUP HAS MEMBERS BOARD AND SEIZE U.S. FLIGHTS. THEY SLAM THE

AIRPLANES INTO THE WORLD TRADE
CENTER AND THE PENTAGON.
12 TONS OF GOLD USED FOR THE
NEW YORK GOLD TRADE ARE BURIED
AT THE BOTTOM OF THE WORLD
TRADE CENTER RUBBLE. MOST OF
THE PEOPLE RUNNING THE U.S. BOND
MARKET ARE KILLED. ANTHRAX SPORE
BEGINS TO BE MAILED TO LEADING
NEWS PERSONALITIES AND U.S.
CONGRESSMEN. AS THE YEAR ENDS THE
U.S. BOND MARKET BEGINS SHOWING
STRESS SIGNS. RUSSIA, CHINA, AND
ISRAEL EXPERIENCE BULL STOCK
MARKETS WHILE THE U.S. AND THE
REST OF THE WORLD HAVE ENTERED
BEAR MARKETS.
THE U.S. HAS FINANCED THE RUSSIAN
ECONOMY REBOUND. RUSSIA AND
CHINA CONTINUE TO BUILD THEIR
MILITARIES FOR EXPECTED CONFLICT
WITH THE U.S. CHINESE GENERALS
HAVE WRITTEN THAT BEFORE YOU
INVADE OR BEGIN A WAR WITH
YOUR ENEMY, YOU FIRST DESTROY
HIS ECONOMY. J.P. MORGAN/CHASE
BANK COMPLEX, A CLINTON AID IN
DISPOSING OF THE U.S. GOLD WEALTH,
IS HEDGED 712 TIMES ITS NET WORTH
AGAINST GOLD AND RISING INTEREST
RATES. THEY ARE SET TO BE A TRIGGER
FOR U.S. ECONOMIC COLLAPSE. ENRON
ENTERS BANKRUPTCY CHARGING OFF
2.6 BILLION IN UNSECURED DEBT
TO JP MORGAN/CHASE. J.P. MORGAN
SEEMS TO GET RID OF MOST OF ITS
GOLD DERIVATIVES WITH THE ENRON
COLLAPSE. RECORDS ARE SHREDDED
AND FEW WILL EVER KNOW FOR SURE

WHAT HAPPENED. ARGENTINA ENTERS
BANKRUPTCY CHARGING OFF SEVERAL
BILLION MORE TO THE SAME BANK
COMPLEX. THEY ARE LEVERAGED OUT
WITH LIABILITIES OVER 20 TRILLION
AND A NORMAL NET PROFIT OF LESS
THAN 6 BILLION PER YEAR. THEIR
TENTACLES STRETCH THROUGHOUT
THE U.S. BANKING SYSTEMS.

2002 A.D.   SAM SIAM, MOSES, AND BILL SINGLETON
WORK TOGETHER PIECING OUT
BUDDHA'S RELATIONSHIP WITH
DANIEL. SAM SIAM HAS BEEN A
CHAINGMAI THAILAND TRAINED
BUDDHIST MONK. MOSES WAS
FORMERLY A LEADER OF BUDDHIST
MONKS AND TRAINED TWELVE YEARS
IN CAMBODIA'S BUDDHIST UNIVERSITY
SYSTEM. SAM AND MOSES BOTH
CURRENTLY PREACH ABOUT JESUS.
GOD HAS PROVIDED UNDERSTANDING
ABOUT HIS PREPARATION OF THE
PEOPLES OF ASIA FOR MASS AND RAPID
EVANGELISM TO THE CHRISTIAN FAITH.
HE HAS BLESSED US WITH A MARVELOUS
TOOL FOR THE CONVERSION OF THE
BUDDHISTS. HE HAD BUDDHA ORDER
THEM TO LEAVE THEIR OLD WAYS AND
JOIN US WHEN WE COME.
WHY THE CHRISTIAN MOVEMENT
HASN'T UNCOVERED THIS BEFORE
NOW IS BEYOND ME EXCEPT FOR GOD'S
TIMING. WHAT A WONDER GOD HAS
PROVIDED FOR OUR TIMES!!! MOSES
TRAVELS CAMBODIA DURING JANUARY
AND FEBRUARY BAPTIZING OVER 150
INTO CHRIST.
THE ELECTION IN FEBRUARY
INCREASES SAM RAINSY
CONTROL OF LOCAL POLITICS TO

OVER 20%. THE KING'S POWER DROPS TO AROUND 20%. IN THE U.S.THE FOREIGN CURRENCY EXCHANGE MARKET IS OPENED UP TO ENABLE SMALL BUSINESSES AND INDIVIDUALS TO PARTICIPATE. PAULEY STARTS TEACHING HIS COMMUNITY IN HIS HOME. BILL SINGLETON, MOSES AND BILL SMITH START A RADIO PROGRAM THAT EXPLAINS SI-A-METREY TO THE BUDDHIST WORLD. .

2003 A.D.   THE LEAD BUDDHIST AND MOSLEMS OF POUTHISAT PROVINCE ASK FOR A HEARING OF THE GOSPEL. THEY GATHER ALMOST 3000 OF THEIR LEADERS FOR THE HEARING AND 387 ARE BAPTIZED. BILL SINGLETON, SAMOL SETH (MOSES) AND BILL SMITH HAVE BEEN BROADCASTING THE COMMAND OF BUDDHA TO LEAVE THE OLD WAYS AND BECOME A CHRISTIAN WHEN THE CHRISTIANS COME. NOW THE PEOPLE OF CAMBODIA ARE BEGINNING TO RESPOND. THE HEAD MOSLEM CLERIC OF POUTHISAT PROVINCE IS AMONG THOSE BAPTIZED. HE GOES HOME AND BAPTISES A 600 MEMBER MOSQUE. THERE IS NO ONE TO HELP TEACH AND FOLLOW UP AND THIS CREATES PROBLEMS. FOR FOUR MONTHS MOSLEM COMMUNITIES BEGIN STRUGGLING, TRYING TO HOLD CHRISTIAN SERVICES WITHOUT GUIDANCE. LARGE NUMBERS ARE ALSO BAPTIZED IN OTHER PROVINCES. EARLY IN THE YEAR, BOB BERARD, AT THE REQUEST OF BILL SINGLETON, VISITS KOH DACH AND BAPTIZE OVER 30 MEETING AT PAULEY'S HOME. BOB

PROVIDES CONTINUING TEACHING FOR
THE KOH DACH CHURCH.
IN AUGUST BOB BERARD, MISSIONARY
LEADING THE PHNOM PENH CHURCH
OF CHRIST AND PREACHER'S SCHOOL, IS
KILLED IN A TRAFFIC ACCIDENT WHILE
TRYING TO BRING BIBLE LESSONS
TO DISTANT CHURCHES OF CHRIST
(KOH DACH AND KAMPONG THOM)
ON SUNDAY. SUNSET BIBLE INSTITUTE
SERIOUSLY BEGINS CONSIDERING THE
SET-UP OF A CAMBODIAN SCHOOL FOR
PREACHERS. WE HAVE BEEN ASKING
FOR THIS SINCE 2001. THE COUSIN-
IN-LAW OF THE KING OF CAMBODIA
OFFERS HER PHNOM PENH HOME AND
A CAR AND DRIVER TO FACILITATE
THIS. THE THREE STAR GENERAL THAT
ADVISES THE CAMBODIAN DEFENSE
MINISTER , SI SUN TECH, COMES TO
STOCKTON TO DISCUSS HELPING
EVANGELIZE THE MILITARY. THE HEAD
OF VOCATIONAL EDUCATION AROUND
BATTAMBANG, A ONE STAR GENERAL
AT KAMPONG THOM, AND THE   HEAD
OF PROFESSIONAL EDUCATION IN THE
NORTHERN HALF OF THE COUNTRY
BECOME CHRISTIANS.
GENERAL PRUM PHENG, COMMANDER
OF THE CAMBODIAN ARMY'S
FIRST DIVISION ASKS FOR A
GOSPEL PRESENTATION FOR HIS
3,000-4,000 TROOPS. THIS IS NEVER
ACCOMPLISHED.
THE DOLLAR BEGINS A CONTINUOUS
SLIDE IN VALUE. GOLD BREAKS ABOVE
$400/OUNCE AND SILVER GOES FROM
$4.50 TO $6.90/OUNCE. THE US DOLLAR
IS LOOSING ITS INTERNATIONAL

RESERVE CURRENCY STATUS. THE
GENERAL STOCK MARKET HAS A
SLOW BUT CONTINUOUS RALLY FROM
SHORTLY AFTER THE INVASION OF IRAQ
ON. US LED ALLIANCE INVADES IRAQ.
CHINA OPENS UP A GOLD MARKET AND
PERMITS IT CITIZENS TO PURCHASE
GOLD.

2004 A.D.   DURING JANUARY OVER 500, INCLUDING
TWO GENERALS, ARE BAPTIZED IN
CAMBODIA. A MEETING AT KOH DACH
HAS OVER 250 IN ATTENDANCE AND 30
BAPTISMS.

MISSIONARIES INSIDE CHINA ASK
ABOUT THE SOURCE OF THE SI-A-
MEETREY INFORMATION AND IF IT HAS
BEEN TRANSLATED INTO CHINESE. BILL
SINGLETON TELLS THEM IT HAS NOT
BEEN TRANSLATED AND PUBLISHED IN
CHINESE, PROVIDES THEM WITH AN
ARTICLE ABOUT IT AND ASKS THEM TO
TRANSLATE.

A BUDDHIST COLONY INSIDE
CHINA ASKS TO HEAR ABOUT THE
FULFILLMENT OF THE SI-A-MEETREY
PREDICTIONS AND THE GOSPEL. NAREN
LOR, COUSIN-IN-LAW TO THE KING
OF CAMBODIA, IS SPONSORING TWO
CHURCHES OF CHRIST AND WANTS
TO SPONSOR MORE. PAULEY, CHUNA
SINGLETON'S BROTHER, AN ELDER OF
THE KOH DACH CHURCH OF CHRIST,
AND HIS RELATIVES ESTABLISH TWO
MORE CONGREGATIONS AT TONLEBET
AND VIEL REIGN. A GROUP OF CHARLES
SINGLETON'S FRIENDS IN AND AROUND
PORTALES, N.M. BECOME THE CENTER
OF THE FINANCIAL SUPPORT FOR
THE PAULEY/SINGLETON CAMBODIAN

OUTREACH. CHARLES IS THE FATHER
OF BILL AND LEADS A JAIL MINISTRY
IN PORTALES AND CLOVIS, N.M. IN
2010 HE IS 86 YEARS OLD. JAMES LORK
CONTINUES THE WORK OF BOB BERARD
AT THE PHNOM PENH CHURCH OF
CHRIST, SUPPLYING A SOURCE OF BIBLE
TRAINED TEACHERS. THE CENTRAL
CHURCH OF CHRIST IN STOCKTON,
CA. COMMITS TO SPONSORING JOHN
SPROUL TO GO TO CAMBODIA IN 2005.
AT THE CLOSE OF 2004 A.D. LIM SRENG
ATTENDS A LEADERSHIP GATHERING OF
CAMBODIAN MOSLEMS. HE HAS BEEN
A LEADER IN THE MOSLEM MOVEMENT
TO CHRIST AND IS NEPHEW OF THE
MOSLEM CLERIC BAPTIZED IN 2003
THAT THEN BAPTIZED A 600 MEMBER
MOSQUE. THAT CLERIC HAD BEEN
OPPOSED BY A NUMBER OF MOSLEM
LEADERS WITH EVEN A HANDGERNADE
THROWN IN HIS FRONT YARD. DURING
THAT MEETING THE LEADER OF
THOSE OPPOSING THE SPREAD OF THE
TEACHINGS OF CHRIST IN CAMBODIA
COMES TO LIM SRENG AND ASKS TO
HAVE HIS SON TAUGHT ABOUT JESUS.
AFTER THIS EVENT AL-QAIDA SEEMS TO
QUIT VISITING CAMBODIA.
AN AREA WIDE POLITICAL GATHERING
AMONG SOUTHEAST ASIAN STATES
IS ALSO HELD AT THE END OF 2004.
AT THAT MEETING THE SUBJECT OF
U.S. MISSIONARIES IS BROUGHT UP.
A CAMBODIAN GENERAL STANDS UP
AND TELLS THE GROUP THEY HAVE
BEEN DEALING WITH THE AMERICAN
MISSIONARIES INCORRECTLY. HE SAYS
THE PROPER WAY TO WORK WITH

THEM IS TO LET THEM COME, PREACH,
CONVERT WHOEVER WANTS TO BE
CONVERTED. AS THEY WORK THEY
WILL LIFT UP THE WHOLE ECONOMY.
THE GENERAL FURTHER STATES
THAT HE HAS CHOSEN TO BECOME
CHRISTIAN HIMSELF. AS A RESULT OF
THIS LAOS REVERSES ITS OPPOSITION
TO AMERICAN MISSIONARIES. THE
SAM RAINSY PARTY WINS ABOUT 25-
30% OF THE SEATS IN THE CAMBODIAN
CONGRESS. HUN SEN AND RANARRIDH
AGREED TO DECLARE THE SAM RANSY
PARTY A TERRORIST GROUP AND
SEIZED THEIR SEATS GIVING THEM TO
RANARRIDH'S PARTY. HUN SEN'S PARTY
ALREADY HELD ABOUT 65% OF THE
SEATS. THE HUN SEN GOVERNMENT
SEEMS TO CLEAR THEIR MOVE AGAINST
SAM RANSY WITH CHINA.

2005A.D.   NORODOM SIHANOUK PLACES
HIS SON, SIHAMONI, ON THE
THROWN. RANARRIDH WAS THE
HEIR APPARENT, BUT THERE
SEEMS TO BE FAMILY CONFLICT
OVER HUN SEN AND RANARRIDH'S
MOVE AGAINST SAM RANSY. THE
CONGREGATIONS SPONSORED IN
CAMBODIA THROUGH BILL SINGLETON
REACH TWELVE AS NOREA HOUT, AT
BILL'S REQUEST, GOES TO BATDAMBANG
TO ORGANIZE CONGREGATIONS USING
PREVIOUSLY BAPTIZED GROUPS.
IN JUNE 257 ARE BAPTIZED INTO
CHRIST THROUGH THE EFFORTS OF
THE PAULEY/SINGLETON GROUP. CHEN
LEN LAM AND SOKOM HUN ASKS TO
BE CONSIDERED PART OF THE PAULEY,

BILL SINGLETON OUT REACH TEAM IN CAMBODIA.
THE WOODARD PARK CAMBODIAN CONGREGATION IN FRESNO, CA. (CHEN LEN LAM'S SUPPORT GROUP) BEGIN CARING FOR NOREA HOUT AND THE CONGREGATIONS HE ESTABLISHED IN THE BATDAMBANG AREA.
SOKHOM HUN AND HIS DALLAS, TEXAS CAMBODIAN CHURCH OF CHRIST BEGIN SUPPORTING THE TANGKOK CHURCH GROUP THROUGH PAULEY/BILL SINGLETON. BILL SINGLETON TRAVELS AN AMERICAN ENCAMPMENT CIRCUIT SHARING INFORMATION ABOUT THE CAMBODIAN OUTREACH AND ASKING FOR HELP.
THE HUGHSON, CA. CHURCH OF CHRIST BEGINS FUNCTIONING AS THE SPONSORING CONGREGATION FOR THE PAULEY/BILL SINGLETON CAMBODIAN OUTREACH. ANH PAULEY BAPTIZES THREE ARJAHS, THE TEACHING LEADERSHIP OF TWO BUDDHIST TEMPLES, INTO CHRIST.
CHINA TALKS ABOUT DE-LINKING ITS CURRENCY FROM THE U.S. DOLLAR AND IRAN, RUSSIA AND CHINA BEGIN TO ATTEMPT TO UNDO THE DOLLAR-PETRO SYSTEM SUPPORTING THE US DOLLAR. CHINA BELIEVES BEFORE YOU MAKE WAR ON A COUNTRY YOU MUST FIRST DESTROY THEM FINANCIALLY.
JOHN SPROUL LOCATES AT PHENOM PENH IN OCTOBER. NORODOM AND SIHAMONI SPEND NORODOM'S BIRTHDAY IN BEIJING. NORODOM SIHANOUK IS REPORTED TO HAVE CANCER. BOTH BEAR VALLEY BIBLE

INSTITUTE AND SUNSET BEGIN EFFORTS TO ESTABLISH SCHOOLS OF PREACHING IN CAMBODIA. TRUMAN SCOTT AND CHRIS SWINSFORD LEAD THIS EFFORT AT SUNSET. DENNY PETRILLO, RALPH WILLIAMS, AND DAVID HAMERICK LEAD IT FOR BEAR VALLEY.

2006-2010 A.D. PROJECTIONS OF THE EFFECTS OF THE AIDS PLAGUE SUGGESTS THAT BY THESE DATES, IN ZIMBABWE, OVER 2/3RDS OF THE WOMEN OF CHILDBEARING AGE AND THEIR CHILDREN WILL BE DEAD. THE MELROSE CHURCH OF CHRIST BECOMES THE SPONSORING CONGREGATION FOR THE BILL SINGLETON/PAULEY EFFORT, WHICH CONTINUES TO BAPTIZE OVER ONE/ DAY. HUGHSON CHURCH OF CHRIST HAS LOST ITS ELDERSHIP THROUGH DEATH AND RESIGNATION, AND IT IS DESIRED TO HAVE THE WORK HELPED THROUGH THE ADVICE AND LEADERSHIP OF A STRONG ELDERSHIP. HUGHSON HAS BEEN A GREAT ASSET AND FRIEND DURING ITS SERVICE AND WILL ALWAYS BE APPRECIATED FOR ITS SERVICE IN THE CAUSE OF CHRIST. ABOUT THIRTY CONGREGATIONS HAVE BEEN STARTED BY THE GROUP BY THE END OF THIS TIME. PAULEY HAS PERSONALLY BAPTIZED ALMOST 1700 PEOPLE INTO CHRIST. A LEADERSHIP TRAINING PROGRAM BEGINS IN 2006 WITH OVER 30 LEADERS FROM VARIOUS CONGREGATIONS ATTENDING TWO DAY MEETINGS EVERY TWO OR THREE MONTHS IN KAMPONG CHAM. BY 2010 THE ATTENDANCE IS REGULARLY RUNNING

OVER A HUNDRED. CHOEU LORK IS CARING FOR FIVE CONGREGATIONS AROUND PHNOM PENH LEFT BY BOB BERARD AND HAS ADDED TO THAT NUMBER FOUR MORE.

CHAN LORK, CHOEU'S YOUNGER BROTHER, HAS JOINED THE BEAR VALLEY EFFORT IN SIEM REAP AND SEVERAL CONGREGATIONS HAVE BEEN ESTABLISHED THERE. TAWN LORK, ANOTHER LORK BROTHER, IS WORKING WITH SUNSET IN PHNOM PENH AND MAINTAINS A CONGREGATION TO THE WEST OF THE CAPITAL. THE BILL SINGLETON/ PAULEY GROUP IS MAINTAINING A RADIO PROGRAM WITH THE HELP OF "WORLD RADIO" AND "KEY TO THE KINGDOM." IT BROADCASTS THIRTY MINUTS/DAY IN THE KAMPONG CHAM AREA AND THIRTY MINUTES/ DAY NATION WIDE. THEY CENTER IN KAMPONG TOM AND KAMPONG CHAM PROVINCES.

SOKHUM HUN IS FOCUSING ON DEVELOPING THE MOSLEM OUTREACH WITH LIM SRENG (AN EARLY MOSLEM CONVERT AND HIGH RANKING OFFICER WITH THE CAMBODIAN DEPARTMENT OF INTERIOR). CHEN LEN LAM IS DEVELOPING A GROUP AROUND BATDAMBANG AND SOUTHWEST OF PHNOM PENH. OTHERS ARE ALSO ACTIVE IN THE TEN YEAR OLD CAMBODIAN EVANGLISTIC EFFORT OF THE CHURCHES OF CHRIST.

2008 A.D. DURING SEPTEMBER THE U.S. BANKING SYSTEM COMES VERY CLOSE TO FAILURE. EMERGENCY FUNDING

IS APPROVED BY CONGRESS. THE
HUGHSON CHURCH, THROUGH DEATH
AND OLD AGE, HAS LOST ITS ELDERSHIP
AND THE MELROSE CHURCH OF CHRIST
BEGINS SPONSORING THE CAMBODIAN
OUTREACH LEAD BY PAULEY AND
BILL SINGLETON. SEVERAL MORE
CONGREGATIONS ARE ADDED TO THE
WORK.

CHAPTER FOURTEEN
A CHRISTIAN CHRONOLOGY OF HISTORY
(2008 A.D. – 2029 A.D.)
A TIME LINE OF HUMAN HISTORY
FROM A CHRISTIAN PROSPECTIVE
Compiled by "God's Friend"

2008-2010 A.D.   BARRACK HUSAINE OBAMA, AN
                  APPARENT ILLEGAL ALIEN, IS ELECTED
                  PRESIDENT OF THE UNITED STATES.
                  DURING THE ELECTION CAMPAIGN
                  OBAMA HAS AN OVERWHELMING
                  FUNDING ADVANTAGE. AFTER THE
                  ELECTION THE PALESTINIANS AND
                  LIBYA'S MUAMMER GADDAFI CLAIM
                  THEY FINANCED OBAMA'S ELECTION,
                  "BUYING" THE ELECTION FOR HIM.
                  IF THIS IS TRUE IT WAS ILLEGAL.
                  OBAMA HIDES THE SOURCE OF
                  ABOUT $300,000,000.00 IN CAMPAIGN
                  DONATIONS. HE ADMITTED TO NOT
                  BEING A NATIVE BORN AMERICAN
                  IN A DEBATE WITH AMBASADOR
                  KEYES WHEN HE RAN FOR THE U.S.
                  SENATE. KEYES CHALLENGES HIS
                  ELIGIABILITY IN CALIFORNIA COURTS.
                  THE CONSTITUTION, THE HIGHEST
                  SECULAR LAW OF THE LAND, SAYS A
                  PRESIDENT MUST BE A NATIVE BORN
                  CITIZEN OF THE UNITED STATES.
                  THAT CASE IS DELAYED FOR MONTHS
                  AND THEN THE JUDGE REFUSES TO
                  HEAR IT AT THE REQUEST OF THE

U.S. JUSTICE DEPARTMENT. OBAMA POSTS A HAWAIIAN BIRTH CERTIFICATE (DECLARATION OF BIRTH) ON HIS POLITICAL WEB SITE. THIS TYPE OF CERTIFICATE CAN BE FILED BY ANYONE AT ANYTIME AND IS NOT LEGAL FOR MOST OFFICIAL PURPOSES. IT FAILS TO IDENTIFY THE DOCTOR OR HOSPITAL. REPORTEDLY A SOCIAL SECURITY NUMBER USED BY OBAMA IS CHECKED AND FOUND NEVER TO HAVE BEEN USED IN ANY HAWAIIAN HOSPITAL. IT ALSO APPEARS TO REPRESENT AN IDENTITY THEFT. HIS MOTHER'S SOCIAL SECURITY NUMBER IS ALSO CHECKED WITH SIMILAR HOSPITAL RESULTS. REPORTED ANALYSIS SAYS THE BIRTH CERTIFICATE WAS PRINTED ON A PRINTER FIRST MANUFACTURED MANY YEARS AFTER OBAMA'S BIRTH. OBAMA'S PATERNAL GRANDMOTHER SAYS SHE WAS PRESENT AT HIS BIRTH IN KENYA. THE AIRPORT IN NIAROBI, KENYA PUTS UP A WELCOME SIGN IDENTIFYING KENYA AS OBAMA'S BIRTH PLACE. CONGRESSMEN IN THE KENYAN LEGISLATURE EXCHANGE COMMENTS ABOUT AMERICA CHOOSING KENYAN BORN OBAMA AS THEIR PRESIDENT. AN AMERICAN, LUCAS SMITH, TRAVELS TO KENYA AND RETURNS WITH WHAT HE CLAIMS IS A COPY OF OBAMA'S KENYAN BIRTH CERTIFICATE. IT APPEARS MUCH MORE LEGITIMATE THAN THE ONE POSTED BY OBAMA ON HIS POLITICAL WEB. (SEE THE ATTACHED KENYAN BIRTH CERTIFICATE AND LUCAS SMITH'S LEGAL AFFIDAVIT

ABOUT THE SOURCE OF THE BIRTH CERTIFICATE.) IF OBAMA WAS BORN IN KENYA, IT IS UNCONSTITUTIONAL FOR HIM TO HOLD THE OFFICE OF PRESIDENT OF THE UNITED STATES. IT IS CLAIMED OTHERS, UNDER COURT ORDER, HAVE OBTAINED EVIDENCE FROM OCCIDENTAL UNIVERSITY INDICATING HE ATTENDED THAT INSTITUTION AS A FOREIGN NATIONAL. THIS HAPPENS WHILE HE IS AN ADULT, IN HIS TWENTIES. THIS IS BEFORE CITIZENS ARE ALLOWED TO OBTAIN DUAL CITIZENSHIP. IF HE DESERTED HIS AMERICAN CITIZENSHIP TO BECOME A FOREIGN NATIONAL, HE IS LEGALLY BARRED FROM EVER REGAINING THAT CITIZENSHIP.

2010 A.D. THE ONE WHO WON THE HAWAIAN GOVERNORSHIP PLEDGED DURING HIS CAMPAIGN HE WOULD MAKE OBAMA'S LONG FORM BIRTH CERTIFICATE PUBLIC. WHEN HE TRIES TO FULFILL THE PLEDGE, HE FINDS HE CAN NOT FIND AN OBAMA BIRTH CERTIFICATE IN THE STATE RECORDS.

Dr. Orly Taitz, Attorney-at-Law
(California SBN 223433)
Orly Taitz Law Offices
26302 La Paz, Suite 211
Mission Viejo, California 92691
Telephone: (949) 683-5411
E-Mail: dr_taitz@yahoo.com

UNITED STATES DISTRICT COURT
FOR THE CENTRAL DISTRICT OF CALIFORNIA
SANTA ANA (SOUTHERN) DIVISION

Captain Pamela Barnett, et al.,
　　　　　　　Plaintiffs,

　　　　v.

Barack Hussein Obama,
Michelle L.R. Obama,
Hillary Rodham Clinton, Secretary of State,
Robert M. Gates, Secretary of Defense,
Joseph R. Biden, Vice-President and
President of the Senate,
　　　　　　　Defendants.

Civil Action:

SACV09-00082-DOC (Anx)

28 U.S.C. §1746 Declaration of Lucas Daniel Smith

1. My name is Lucas Daniel Smith. I am over 18 years old, am of sound mind and free of any mental disease or psychological impairment of any kind or condition.

2.　I am a citizen of the United States of America, I am 29 years old and I was born in the state of Iowa.

3.　I have personal knowledge of all the facts and circumstances described herein below in this declaration and will testify in open court to all of the same.

4.　On February 19, 2009 I visited the Coast General hospital in Mombasa, Kenya.

5.　I visited the hospital accompanied by one more person, a natural born citizen of the Democratic Republic of Congo (formerly known as

DR. ORLY TAITZ
FOR THE PLAINTIFFS
26302 LA PAZ SUITE 211
MISSION VIEJO CALIFORNIA 92691

148

"Zaire" and before independence as the "Belgian Congo").

6.　I traveled to Kenya and Mombasa in particular with the intent to obtain the original birth certificate of Barack Hussein Obama, as I was told previously that it was on file in the hospital and under seal, due to the fact that the prime minister of Kenya Raela Odinga is Barack Hussein Obama's cousin.

7.　I had to pay a cash "consideration" to a Kenyan military officer on duty to look the other way, while I obtained the copy of the birth certificate of Barack Hussein Obama.

8.　The copy was signed by the hospital administrator.

9.　The copy contain the embossed seal.

10.　The true and correct photocopy of the Birth certificate obtained, is attached to this affidavit as Exhibit A.

11.　I declare, certify, verify, state, and affirm under penalty of perjury under the laws of the United States of America that the foregoing statements of fact and descriptions of circumstances and events are true and correct.

12.　I have not received any compensation for making this affidavit.

Further, Declarant saith naught.

Signed and executed in on this 3rd day of September, 2009.

By: _____
Lucas Daniel Smith

DR. ORLEY TAITZ
FOR THE PLAINTIFFS
26302 LA PAZ SUITE 211
MISSION VIEJO, CALIFORNIA 92691

149

COAST PROVINCE GENERAL HOSPITAL

Mombasa, British Protectorate of Kenya

CERTIFICATE OF BIRTH

Certificate No. 32018

BARACK HUSSEIN OBAMA II   / Sex M

was born to

STANLEY ANN OBAMA   DUNHAM   11/29/1942
Full Name of Mother   Maiden Surname   Date of Birth

BARACK HUSSEIN OBAMA   1936
Full Name of Father   Date of Birth

on the 4th day of AUGUST, 1961   at 7:24 PM

7 pounds 1 ounce   18 inches   6 inches
Weight of Child at Birth   Length   Width Between Shoulders

HONOLULU, HAWAII,   WICHITA, KANSAS,
UNITED STATES   UNITED STATES
Residence of Mother   Birth Place of Mother

KANYADHIANG VILLAGE, NYANZA   STUDENT   STUDENT
Birth Place of Father   Occupation of Father   Occupation of Mother

JAMES O. W. ANG'AWA   8/8/1961
Name of Attending Doctor   Signature of Doctor   Date

JOHN KWAME ODONGO
Registrar of Chronicles

8-7-1961
Signature   Date

150

SOME OBAMA SUPPORTERS HAVE
CRITICISED THE ABOVE CERTIFICATE
BECAUSE THEY SAY MOMBASA DID
NOT BECOME PART OF KENYA UNTIL
DECEMBER 1963, WHEN IT WAS CEDED
BY ZANZIBAR. THIS IGNORES HOSPITAL
ADMINISTRATIVE RECORDS. THE
MOBASA HOSPITAL WAS ESTABLISED
IN 1891 WHEN THE IMPERIAL BRITISH
EAST AFRICA COMPANY RECEIVED A
DONATION TO BUILD A HOSPITAL.
ONLY THREE YEARS EARLIER THEY HAD
RECEIVED THEIR OWN CHARTER FROM
QUEEN VICTORIA. THE RUNNING OF
THE HOSPITAL WAS GIVEN TO THE HOLY
GHOST FATHERS OF THE CATHOLIC
CHURCH. GOVERNMENTAL OVERSITE
OF THE HOSPITAL WAS UNDER THE
EAST AFRICA BRITISH PROTECTORATE.
AT THAT TIME THE HEADQUARTERS OF
THE PROTECTORATE WAS IN MOMBASA,
BUT LATER MOVED TO NAIROBI IN
1907. IN 1920 THE EAST AFRICA BRITISH
PROTECTORATE BECAME THE KENYA
COLONY AND PROTECTORATE. THE
BRITISH APPOINTED GOVERNOR OF
THE KENYA PROTECTORATE EVEN
HAD THE MOBASA HOSPITAL NURSES
LIVING IN HIS GOVERNMENT HOME
FACILITY FROM 1944 TO 1952. THE
HOSPITAL WAS ADMINISTERED AND
STAFFED BY CATHOLIC NUNS AND
PRIESTS. IT WAS INITIALLY ONLY FOR
THE EUROPEAN POPULATION, THOUGH
LATER ITS SERVICE WAS EXTENDED TO
AFRICANS. IT WAS NEVER UNDER THE
GOVERNMENT OF THE MOSLEM SULTAN
OF ZANZIBAR, WHOSE RELIGIOUS
STANDARD, THE QURAN, ENDORSES

AND APPROVES OF THE RAPE AND
MURDER OF CHRISTIAN WOMEN.
CALL IT COLONIAL ARROGANCE OR
PERSONNAL SURVIVAL, THE NUNS
AND CATHOLIC PRIESTS, WHO
SUPERVISED AND STAFFED THE MOBASA
HOSPITAL, WERE ALWAYS UNDER THE
GOVERNMENTAL PROTECTION OF
THE BRITISH CROWN, UNTIL THE
DAY THEY WERE PLACED UNDER THE
REPUBLIC OF KENYA. THE IDENTIFIED
GOVERNMENT AUTHORITY ON THE
BIRTH CERTIFICATE OFFERED BY LUCAS
SMITH IS THE CORRECT GOVERNMENT
AUTHORITY FOR THE MOBASSA COAST
PROVINCE GENERAL HOSPITAL AT
THE DATE OF THE BIRTH OF OBAMA.
IT IS REPORTED THAT THIS HOSPITAL
HAD THE BEST MATERNITY WARD IN
THE REGION AT THE TIME OF OBAMA'S
BIRTH.

THAT SHOULD BE A REASON
FOR ACCEPTANCE AND NOT THE
FALLACIOUS CHALLENGE BEING
VOICED BY DEMOCRATES. IN ADDITION
IT IS NOW REPORTED THAT THREE
ADDITIONAL INDIVIDUALS HAVE
RECEIVED CERTIFIED COPIES OF THE
SAME BIRTH CERTIFICATE FOR OBAMA
FROM KENYA.

OBAMA DOES NOT HOLD THE VISA
REQUIRED TO LEGALIZE THE PRESENCE
OF A FOREIGN NATIONAL IN THE
UNITED STATES. THEREFORE, IT
APPEARS MOST LIKELY HE IS AN ILLEGAL
ALIEN. IT ALSO SEEMS PROBABLE THAT

HE HOLDS THE OFFICE OF PRESIDENT
THROUGH FRAUD AND DECEPTION.

OBAMA HAS FURTHER COURT
MARSHALLED AN OUTSTANDING
MILITARY OFFICIER, LTC TERRY
LAKIN, DENYING HIM DISCOVERY
RIGHTS DURING HIS TRIAL. LTC LAKIN
RESPONSIBLY SOUGHT PROOF THAT
OBAMA WAS A CONSTITUTIONAL
PRESIDENT. INSTEAD OF DISCOVERY
RIGHTS, LTC LAKIN WAS IMPRISONED.
HIS COURT MARTIAL MAKES AN
OXYMORON OUT OF THE TERM,
"MILITARY JUSTICE." THE GUILTY IS
GOING FREE AND THE COURAGEOUS
PATRIOT STANDING UP FOR THE
CONSTITUTION IS INCARCERATED.
THERE WAS A TIME WHEN RESPONSIBLE
MILITARY AUTHORITIES UNDERSTOOD
SOLDIERS HAD A DUTY AND RIGHT
TO ASSURE THEMSELVES THAT THEIR
ORDERS CAME FROM A VALID SOURCE.
THEY UNDERSTOOD OFFICERS HAD
THE DUTY TO CONFIRM THIS WHEN
THERE WAS REASONABLE DOUBT. THERE
IS CERTAINLY REASONABLE DOUBT
THAT OBAMA IS A CONSTITUTIONAL
PRESIDENT.

OBAMA VERBALLY CLAIMS TO BE A
CHRISTIAN WHEN SPEAKING TO THE
AMERICAN VOTERS, BUT HIS ACTIONS
SPEAK MUCH LOUDER THAN HIS
WORDS. HE ALSO TALKS ABOUT HIS
"MOSLEM FAITH", WHEN AWAY FROM
THE STATES, ORDERED BIBLES BURNED
IN AFGHANISTAN, OBJECTED TO THE
BURNING OF A QURAN IN FLORIDA,

ORDERED NAVY CROSSES REMOVES
FROM ARLINGTON CEMETARY AND
THE HISTORIC RECORD OF THOSE
CROSSES ERASED, USES TAX DOLLARS
TO BUILD MOSQUES, AND FINANCED
THE TRAVEL OF A MOSLEM CLERIC TO
RECRUIT SUPPORT FOR THE BUILDING
OF A MOSQUE AT GROUND ZERO IN
NEW YORK. HE ALSO HELPS TO IMPORT
MOSLEMS FROM INDONESIA, SOMALIA
AND PALESTINE INTO THE UNITED
STATES. HE REFUSES TO PROTECT THE
U.S. BORDER AND IS ATTEMPTING TO
GIVE THOSE RECENTLY BROUGHT INTO
THE UNITED STATES U.S. CITIZENSHIP
AND VOTING RIGHTS.

HE IS ALSO ATTEMPTING TO REMOVE
THE RIGHT TO HAVE FIRE ARMS AND
HAS INCLUDED IN THE HEALTH
CARE BILL A MEASURE TO LET HIM
FORM, ARM, TRAIN, AND EQUIP A
SEVERAL THOUSAND MAN ARMY
FOR HIS PERSONAL USE INSIDE THE
CONTINENTAL UNITED STATES.

HE HAS OPENLY TRIED TO INTIMIDATE
THE JUSTICES OF THE SUPREME COURT
WITH EMPEACHMENT, CONSTANTLY
RIDICULES THE USE OF CHRISTIAN
INFLUENCE IN THE CREATION OF
LAWS, AND INDICATES THE U.S.
CONSTITUTION SHOULD BE IGNORED.

IN NOVEMBER 2008, WHEN I RETURNED
TO CAMBODIA, KAMPONG CHAM WAS
FULL OF MOSLEMS FROM MALAYSIA,
INDONESIA, AND SOMALIA, CLAIMING
OBAMA HAD PROMISED THAT THEY

COULD MOVE TO THE UNITED STATES.
THEY WERE FILLING OUT FORMS
AND THEN DISAPPEARING INTO THE
COUNTRYSIDE WHILE ANOTHER WAVE
CAME IN TO FILL OUT THE IMIGRATION
FORMS. KAMPONG CHAM IS NOT A
CENTER FOR FILLING OUT FORMS
FOR IMIGRATION, BUT THAT YEAR IT
WAS. THE MOSLEMS WERE REPORTING
THAT THEY EXPECTED TO LIVE IN THE
COUNTRYSIDE FOR A YEAR BEFORE
OBAMA WOULD GET THEM ENTRANCE
INTO THE UNITED STATES. THERE WAS
A NEW WAVE EVERY FOUR DAYS. THE
MOSLEMS SEEMED TO BE ALMOST ALL
MALES. THE YOUNGER ONES CLAIMED
TO BE RADIOLOGICAL EXPERTS,
BUT AN OLDER MAN SAID HE WAS A
COMMANDER OF A SOMALI MALITIA.
MY IMPRESSION WAS THE OLDER MAN
WAS THE ONLY ONE BEING TRUTHFUL.
THE YOUNGER ONES SEEMED TO
KNOW PRACTICALLY NO SCIENCE AND
WOULD QUICKLY CHANGE THE SUBJECT
OR LEAVE IF YOU TRIED TO DISCUSS
SCIENTIFIC SUBJECTS RELATED TO
THEIR CLAIMED FIELD OF EXPERTISE.

2009 A.D.   OTHO ROGERS AND BUTCH CROZIER
OF THE MELROSE CHURCH VISITED
CAMBODIA. WITH PAULEY'S HELP THEY
HELD A TWO DAY TEACHING SESSION
FOR TEN DENOMINATIONAL
CONGREGATIONS WITH 50 LEADER IN
ATTENDANCE. THEY THEN TRAINED
OVER EIGHTY CHURCH OF CHRIST
LEADERS IN A TWO DAY MEETING.
MORE CONGREGATIONS ARE BEING
STARTED BY THE GROUP THE MELROSE
CHURCH HELPS FINANCE.

(SEE MORE IN THE NEXT EDITION, LORD WILLING.)
(PRAY FOR AMERICA AND ITS CITIZENS' INALIENABLE
RIGHTS. MAY THESE BE MAINTAINED WITHOUT
INTERNAL MILITARY CONFLICT.)

IF YOU WOULD LIKE TO HELP
THE CAMBODIAN MISSION MENTIONED IN
THESE PAGES FOLLOWING 2000 A.D.,
PLEASE CONTACT OR SEND HELP TO:

**CAMBODIAN MISSIONS
MELROSE CHURCH OF CHRIST
340 NORTH 8TH ST.
MELROSE, N.M. 88124**

BECAUSE OF FEAR AND INTIMIDATION THE CHRISTIANS
HAVE TENDED TO FAIL TO EVANGELIZE THE MOSLEMS.
NOW GOD IS PERMITTING THEM TO ENTER OUR
INCUBATOR. IF WE WISH TO LIVE LIVES WITHOUT HEAVY,
LIFE THREATENING PERSECUTION, WE MUST EVANGELIZE.
THIS IS SOMETHING WE SHOULD HAVE BEEN DOING ALL
ALONG. THE QURAN TELLS THEM THAT JESUS IS THE ONLY
ONE THAT CAN FORGIVE SINS (Surah Al-lmran 3:42-55). THEY
ARE NOT STUPID, BUT ARE VERY RELIGIOUS. THEY ARE
IMPROPERLY ZEALOUS LIKE THE FIRST CENTURY JEWS WHO
PERSECUTED CHRISTIANS. POINT OUT THAT THEIR SINS
ARE WHAT WILL DENY THEM ENTRY INTO HEAVEN AND IF
JESUS IS THE ONLY ONE THAT CAN SOLVE THAT PROBLEM,
THEY NEED TO KNOW ABOUT HIM AND HIS PLAN OF
SALVATION. OUR SUCCESS AT EVANGELIZING THEM IS THE
ONLY THING THAT IS LIKELY TO MAKE AMERICA SAFE FOR
OUR CHILDREN AND GRANDCHILDREN. THEIR RELIGION
IS ONE OF HATE. WE MUST SHOW THEM A BETTER WAY
(ROMANS 12:19-21).

ABOUT THE AUTHOR

God's Friend was education at many of our nation's very best colleges and universities. He did undergraduate work at Lubbock Christian University, the University of New Mexico and Abilene Christian University. He received his B.S.E. from A.C.U. in Biology and Chemistry, placing in the top one percentile on the National Teachers' Examination, among graduates specializing in Biology and Science. After a tour in Vietnam and five military medals, he returned to do graduate work in Biology at New Mexico Highlands University. During five years as a Food and Drug Investigator he received further science oriented training at Temple Buell College, The University of Wisconsin, The University of Rhode Island, Denver Metro State College, The University of Idaho, and Cornell University. He then attended the Preston Road School of Preaching, graduating and doing graduate work in Bible related studies at Pepperdine University. Education and science related graduate work was also completed at California State at Stanislaus.

He has been responsible for all F.D.A. operations in Montana and a third of all operations in a six state region.

He has filled the pulpits of many of the churches of Christ. He has been a full time pulpit minister for the Singing Oaks church of Christ in Denton, Texas and the Livermore Church of Christ in Livermore, California. He preached for over eight years for the Lathrop Church of Christ. He was a volunteer Chaplain for the California Department of Corrections for fifteen years prior to becoming a missionary to Cambodia. He has worked in that country longer than any other missionary in the churches of Christ and he and his converts have established over 30 congregations in 9 years. The group has averaged baptizing over one/day among the Buddhist with the baptism of three arjahwats (teacher leaders of Buddhist temples). His work among the

Moslem population has helped establish 10 congregations there with the baptism of a leading Moslem cleric.

He has been the Science Chair person for two different Science Departments in the Stockton Unified School District. He served many years on the Executive Board of Directors for the Stockton Teachers' Association. His students received more honors in county and state competition of the Science Fairs' than students of any other teacher in the county. As a school teacher he has taught Biology, General Science, Introductory Physical Science, Physical Science, Earth Science, Life Science, History, Math, and Algebra.

He has served on the Board of Directors for five corporations.

His literature efforts have resulted in his work being included in "The Best Poems and Poets of 2003," "2004," and "2005". He has published on three continents in two languages. In recognition of outstanding achievement his biographic sketch has been listed in "Who's Who among America's Teachers," "Who's Who in American Education," and "Who's Who in the West."